DARN RIGHT IT'S BUTCH

MEMORIES OF *OUR GANG* *THE LITTLE RASCALS*

TOMMY "BUTCH" BOND
with RON GENINI

MORGIN PRESS INC.
WAYNE, PA
1994

MORGIN PRESS INC.
303 W. Lancaster Ave. #283
Wayne, PA 19087 U.S.A.

Bond, Thomas R. (1926 —) ; Genini, Ronald W. (1946 —)
    Darn Right It's Butch: Memories Of Our Gang —
    The Little Rascals
        p.   cm.
    ISBN 0-9630976-5-2

Library of Congress Cataloguing-in-Publishing Data
    CIP 93-086222

MORGIN PRESS books are available at special discounts for bulk purchases, for sales promotions, premiums, fund-raising, or educational use. For details contact:
    Special Sales Director
    Morgin Press Inc.
    303 W. Lancaster Ave. #283
    Wayne PA.19087 U.S.A.

Cover Design: Izhar Zik & Barbara Solot. Graphics V, Philadelphia
Cover Photographs Courtesy King World Productions, Inc.
Book Design and Layout: Ann Maloney
Editing: Caslon, Inc.
Proofreader: Jennifer Baldino
Printed and Bound by: Maple-Vail Press Co.

First Edition
10 9 8 7 6 5 4 3 2

Acknowledgments

I would like to acknowledge those whose lives have touched mine and who have helped me reach this point. Most of them are still with us but some have passed away. I hope that their families will know that I remembered them.

Special thanks go to my son, Thomas Bond II, who inspired me with enthusiasm and added literary assistance to this book. I would like to acknowledge Dave Andrews, Ron Appling, John Bakus, Richard Bann, Joe Bernay, Phil Beuth, Walt Bingilli, Dale Blickenstaff, Al Case, Bill Cassera, Tom Castelazo, Chuck Coon, Joanne Corliss, John Douglas, Dennis DuPriest, Andy Edmonds, Marc Edwards, Fernando Granado, Sharry Han, Everett and Betsy Henderson, Chuck Hudelson, Lee Jason, Joe Kaufenberg, Walt Liss, Allan Ludden, Leonard Maltin, Jeff Margolis, Jack Mason, Phil and Phyllis McCoy, Rev. Armand Miller, Jim Myers, Virginia O'Brien, Chip Pashayan, Don Postles, Dr. Marcus and Marcella Rabwin, Al Radka, Lee Reem, Robbie Robinson, Rich Rodriguez, Gene Ross, Bob Satterfield, Greg Saunders, Norm and Norma Scroggins, Ken Sharp, Jack Shea, Jack Simon, Dr. Robb Smith, Sr., Mort Smith, Angelo Stalis, Ed and Vonnie Sturgeon, Peggy Sullivan, Bill Thomas, Jr., Rudy Treviño, Bob Tyrcha, Bob Versace, Betty White, Al Wittnebert, and Rev. Erling and Marge Wold. Not to be forgotten are the staff of Valley Medical Center's burn unit for the unstinting help they gave my family.

Ken Sharp is acknowledged for his unselfish, unremitting assistance in getting this book into print. It was a labor of love for him. He was diligent and untiring with his encouragement and suggestions.

Others who deserve recognition for their efforts in the creation of this book are: Roberta Genini, Don Postles, Kathy Barberich (of the *Fresno Bee*), Randy Skretvedt, and Robert Gropp (of Central Unified School District), who graciously consented to proofread the manuscript. Robert Gropp is deserving of additional mention for his professional assistance with the photographs which grace this work and for generously contributing his time. Randy Skretvedt also added many generally forgotten historical details.

If I have omitted anyone deserving mention, it was due to forgetfulness and was not intentional.

T.B.

I wish to thank Lynne Wilcox Alkire, Alison Claveau Gagnon, Lori Robin Jacobs, Alice Stamm, Charles DiMaria and Cathie Allegra, Kristin Mooney, Teresa Hamann, Theresa Lee, and Linda Woeltjen for the constant encouragement they gave me to complete the task — even at times when it seemed insurmountabe. I am also greatful to my co-workers at Central High in Fresno, California, who assisted me with their time: Lynn Ballinger, Paul Birrell, Michael Facciani, Jeff Feramisco, Dennis Fitzpatrick, Jeannie French, Jean Kellner and, Garry Reagan. I appreciate the encouragement of the students at Central High.

I would also like to thank my sons Thomas, Justin, and Nicholas for their patience while I was busy working on the book.

I wish to thank my parents, William and Irma Genini, who allowed me to watch the *Little Rascals* on TV when I was a little boy. I never realized that my childhood dreams of playing with those kids would evolve into being the co-author of one of their autobiographies.

I am grateful to Theda Bara, wherever she is, for bringing Tommy and me together in 1986. I was researching her life when I contacted Tommy about the old days in Hollywood.

R.G.

We wish to thank the owners and staff of Avanté Printshop in Fresno for typesetting the original copy of our book, and David Pontius, Central Unified's former computer guru, for assisting with the transfer of text from system to system.

We are grateful to the following institutions for their assistance: the Academy of Motion Picture Arts and Sciences in Beverly Hills (especially Sam Gill), Fresno County Free Library, California State University at Fresno, the UCLA Library Theater Arts Special Collections, NBC in Burbank, the Screen Actors Guild in Hollywood, and Warner Brothers in Burbank (especially Denise Mayer and Leith Adams).

We wish to thank Columbia Pictures, D.C. Comics, Larry Harmon Pictures Corp., King World Productions Inc., and Universal Pictures for allowing us to use their photographs. We are extremely grateful.

. . . And a special thanks to Morrie Kricun, President of Morgin Press Inc., for believing in this project and making it happen.

T.B.

R.G.

To Polly. Without her I'm nothing. She turned my life around from one going nowhere to one filled with joy and happiness. She sacrificed her career for mine. She's a helpmate and a wife in every sense of the word.
T.B.

To Roberta.
R.G.

DARN RIGHT IT'S BUTCH

MEMORIES OF *OUR GANG* *THE LITTLE RASCALS*

Contents

Off To Hollywood

There I was, five-and-a-half years old, entering the movie mogul's office. Everything looked big: big oak cabinets, deep, plush carpets, and Mr. Roach himself, seated in a big chair behind a huge desk, and smoking a big cigar. But he immediately put me at ease.

"Come on in," he said. "The talent scout mentioned you. You've come all the way from Texas with your grandmother, haven't you?"

"Yes," I replied.

He sized me up. "Do you like to fight?" he asked.

"Yeah."

"Well, do you think you can be a tough guy?"

"Yeah."

He called in his casting director. "Hire him," he said.

That was how I became an actor. Just like that.

This was back in 1932 B.T. — Before Television, when only the movies and acting in "the pictures" were the high road to fortune for photogenic kids. Hal Roach was famous for discovering and employing youthful talent in *Our Gang* films. Thousands applied, few were chosen. And there was I, about to become one of the *Gang*.

How did I get there? How did it all happen?

The story starts several years before and 1,800 miles away. I was born in Baylor Hospital in Dallas on September 16, 1926. It happened at noon, just in time for lunch. Mom was an only child, the granddaughter of a Mississippi plantation family that would have made Scarlett O'Hara green with envy. Unfortunately, the Civil War left them stranded, and the next generation had to work for a living. All that remains of that fabled time is a silver pitcher full of gold coins, probably prewar Yankee mintage, that her family hid from Grant's men.

My dad, Ashley Ross Bond, was born and raised in New York with two brothers and a sister. He was a commercial artist, educated at the Pratt Institute, an art school in New York City. He loved his work, and I remember him bringing it home and working evenings and weekends.

During World War I he was an army lieutenant stationed in San Antonio. That's how he met Mom. You might say the war was instrumental in producing me. During the war he had been in charge of Texan shock troops in France, a bunch of men six feet tall. He was only five feet four inches. They had to lift "Shorty" over the top when they charged. He was shot, mustard gassed, and cut by barbed wire, and ended the war with an infected kidney. But he never gave up. He felt he came out of the war a better man. After five years in the service he was discharged. Though he was a Yankee, he returned to San Antonio, married Mom, and lost no time in starting a family. My sister Jane was born in 1922. I arrived four years later.

Dad was religious. He taught me honesty, truthfulness, patriotism and a respect for others' feelings. He was very emotional. I saw him cry many times, both with joy and sorrow. Without a doubt I felt closer to him than to my mother. There was more warmth between us, and he was always well supplied with good advice.

He loved Mom as much as any man could love a woman. She was a butterfly — a vain, pretty woman who had been spoiled as a child and who remained spoiled as an adult with children of her own.

Neither parent was overly strict with me, though I felt they doted more on Jane. She had greater need of their emotional support than I. After all, I was destined to play Butch, the tough guy. And tough guys don't need support! Right? Well . . .

Mom's parents divorced (they never shared the reasons with me), yet they remained very devoted to their grandchildren. When I was a boy, Grandma Jane Quinn Sauter lived with our family, but Grandpa Charlie Sauter lived in Laredo, Texas. Laredo is on the Mexican border, and each Christmas Grandpa sent my sister and me a package of Mexican treats — pralines, candies, and little straw men. These helped make it a great holiday along with Santa's gifts.

I never met my paternal grandparents due to the distance between us. They had a successful summer resort on Lake Champlain, New York.

Grandpa Sauter was comfortably retired from the Santa Fe Railroad in a Laredo boarding house and visited us on occasion. He was very religious — a staunch Presbyterian teetotaler. This added some humor when I once visited him for a week, because, ironically, he inadvertently introduced me to beer.

When I was about four years old, he took me across the bridge into Mexico. Holding me by the hand, he was somehow oblivious to the Mexican vendors along the streets who handed me little glasses of beer. I proceeded to drink the beer and got zonked. When Grandpa found out, he was MAD! He picked me up, carried me back across the border, brought me home, and carried on with Mom about it. I must have enjoyed the beer, because later I became a committed beer drinker.

Grandma gave me another life-time commitment — the movies. For me they began as a kind of reward. Little boys hate tagging along with women through department stores. Since Jane was in school and they were reluctant to leave me home alone, Mom and Grandma dragged me with them when they went downtown to shop. As compensation, I would be taken to the movies.

Dad was more or less indifferent to movies, but Grandma, Mom, my sister, and I were passionate about them. I used to accompany them to weekly movie marathon showings held in the Dallas theaters. The talkies were a phenomenon so new and exciting that most people could not get enough of them. So the movie houses sometimes screened all the season's top films, four or five of them, continuously from nine in the morning to six in the evening. Kids loved those marathon days. Theaters were becoming air conditioned. They sold popcorn and candy. We didn't have much else to entertain us during the Depression.

Several movies of that era made a deep impression on me. *The Mask of Fu Manchu*, starring Boris Karloff as the insidious villain, was thrilling to a little kid, what with its depiction of tong wars, opium dens, and mysteries of the Orient. *Tiger Shark*, with Edward G. Robinson, was like seeing *Jaws* for the first time. Here was a man in a lifeboat, trying to fish for his survival while sharks followed in his wake. But perhaps the most exciting of those early films was the MGM extravaganza *Ben Hur,* a silent made in 1925 with Ramon Novarro in the title role. All of us, Dad included, went to see this film revival one evening, and it did something for my attitude toward soap. Soap? In the scene where Ben Hur's mother and sister have been stricken with leprosy, bits of flesh peel from their bodies. Horrified, I asked Mom what caused that, and she replied "Filth." Never again did she have to prod me to take a bath or wash behind my ears. In all other respects I was a normal kid, who did things like stealing watermelons from our kindly neighbor, old Mrs. Coffin. She told my mother, who got a little upset with me. When Mom apologized to her, Mrs. Coffin said I had only to ask. But, hey, watermelons were a weakness of mine.

Watermelons played a large part in family reunions, which were a big deal in those days, especially among Texans. At least that's how I remember them. I can recall reunions with lots of crab gumbo, biscuits and gravy, strawberry shortcake — and watermelons. But none of those served came from Mrs. Coffin.

When I was about five, Jane had been taking an acrobatics class for several years at the Newman School of Dance in Dallas. She was about to appear in a program at the school and had been preparing for it for weeks when another member of the cast got sick at the last minute. Mr. Newman asked Mom if I could sing. She told him I had a talent for remembering lyrics and accompanying the song with gestures. After seeing RKO's *Rio Rita,* I sang "Rio Rita, love 'em sweeta" all the way home in the back seat of our car. Desperate to fill out his program, Mr. Newman asked me, "Would you like to sing, Tommy?" To which I answered, "Sure."

That word led to my entertainment debut. Singing like Eddie Cantor, "Potatoes are cheapa, tomatoes are cheapa, now's the time to fall in love," I was a hit. Jane was furious. She got plenty of applause, but she had been training for years, and along came little brother, drafted on the spur of the moment, getting an equal reception — kind of like the New Testament's "first shall be last and last shall be first." Afterward, Mr. Newman tried to encourage Mom to develop my talent, but she didn't seem interested. After all, what was I going to do with imitative singing in Dallas?

She was right about Dallas, but there was a whole other world out there where I might be able to do something with the talent that Mr. Newman had detected — the world of Hollywood.

The war had made me possible by letting Mom and Dad meet, but it may have helped my career, too. You see, before World War I, the British and European movie makers were far ahead of the Americans, even though the motion picture was an American invention. The American greats — Adolph Zukor, D. W. Griffith, Jesse L. Lasky, Cecil B. DeMille, Mack Sennett — were just getting started when the war shut down the foreign studios. The Europeans' setback allowed the Americans to catch up and surpass them. Most of the Americans working in the movie industry had been working in Fort Lee, New Jersey, but others were in Chicago, Hollywood, and Fremont, California. By the time of the Armistice most of the studios had relocated to Hollywood because of its scenery, sunshine and, yes, clean air. One of these was the Hal Roach Studio.

Mr. Roach was born in 1892. Before he was twenty he had been a mule skinner, fish-wagon driver, saloon hand, and Yukon gold miner. In 1912 he went to work for Universal as a stunt man, extra, and bit player in Westerns. Another bit player, Harold Lloyd, persuaded him to open his own studio with a $3,000 inheritance and to produce comedies. Their venture failed. Lloyd went to work for Mack Sennett's Keystone, later to become Roach's rival. Roach went to Essanay, directing Chaplin's lesser comedians who were on the studio payroll but temporarily idle. The Pathé company found him, hired him to shoot some comedies with Lloyd, and the rest is history. Roach re-formed his own company and brought Lloyd back from Keystone. He directed many Lloyd films, including a comedy series called *Phun-Philms*, and turned Lloyd from a Chaplin imitator into a comedy star with his own style. Unlike Mack Sennett, Roach adopted a comedy formula emphasizing story and characters over gags and pratfalls. This made his work attractive to an increasingly sophisticated audience. Greats rolled from Roach's films: Laurel and Hardy, Charley Chase, Thelma Todd, Patsy Kelly — and, after 1922, *Our Gang*.

The *Our Gang* series was undoubtedly among the most successful Roach comedies, predating the enormously popular *Laurel and Hardy* shorts. This was not the first time movie comedies used children as the actors. *The Fox Kiddies* were well established before *Our Gang*, but their format simply spoofed well-known stories and some Fox movies, allowing tight-fisted Fox to reuse some sets. *The Fox Kiddies* films also were longer and generally inane, so that they hardly appealed to adults. Others, issued by Pathé and Educational, were just as feeble. Roach did not resort to fantasy or melodrama for his story lines. He wanted kids who behaved just like kids, doing the things kids did, especially in those days before television, when they had more time on their hands and more incentive to use their imaginations. This appealed to both adults and children. Before he sold the series to MGM in 1938, he had produced 169 of these shorts, and MGM released an additional 52 before ending the series in 1944.

To find youngsters to play regular all-American kids, the type he wanted, Roach employed talent scouts all over the country. One day when I was dressed in my usual downtown outfit of short pants, shirt, little coat, and beanie, and was walking down one of the main Dallas streets with Mom and Grandma, a gentleman approached us.

"Excuse me, ma'am, is that your son?" he asked.

"Yes," Mom replied.

"You know, he has a great face for movies, a great nose," he went on. "I'm a talent scout, representing Hal Roach. I don't know if your boy can act, but I think he has the spark Hal Roach is looking for."

The scout guaranteed an interview with Roach if I could get to California. Mom and Grandma conferred and decided that Grandma would take me to Hollywood.

Grandma knew an agent, P. B. Mahoney, whom she had met when Jane and I attracted his attention at the Newman School performance. Grandma decided to take him with us to promote me at the Roach Studio. Mahoney was no novice at promoting acting careers. He had discovered Joan Blondell in Texas, and we all knew how her screen career had blossomed. A nervous, white-haired gentleman, Mahoney had concluded that Texas wasn't providing show-biz opportunities and had made up his mind to move to California. So, with Mom and Dad's blessings, Grandma, Mr. Mahoney, and I set out across the desert in Grandma's 1931 four-door LaSalle sedan.

It started out as an adventure. Remember, I was just five-and-a-half. I was going to California — not just to California, but to Hollywood, the movie capital. Grandma also treated it as an adventure, but she kept cushioning our high hopes by reminding me, "If it doesn't work out, we'll just come home."

What a depressing ride it turned out to be! The motels

along the road were no more than little huts, fifty cents a night, providing a place to sleep and nothing more. Grandma refused to stop at these run-down shacks and told Mahoney we would drive on through. I could stretch out in the back seat and they would take turns driving.

We went on over the two-lane highways, occasionally hitting stretches of gravel, dirt road, and even the old wood-plank road. We encountered Okie refugees from the dust bowl, loaded in cars and trucks à la *Grapes of Wrath*. And the tarantulas! We drove over a sea of these hairy spiders, popping them until they sounded like popcorn. Rain added another adventure to the journey. The roads would be level, then suddenly dip, and the depressions filled with rain water. Cars sank above the hubcaps in these pools. We came to one such dip at night where Grandma had to detour in first gear around a drowned car.

We finally reached Hollywood after ten rough days on the road. We went to a boarding house on Alvarado Street, on the eastern outskirts of Hollywood. It housed some interesting people. One, a Mr. Sims, a man in his forties, caught barracuda right off the Santa Monica Pier and brought them back for a big fish fry. One thing I hated about the place was that Grandma tried to introduce me to avocados there. I detested them and took mouthfuls to the toilet to spit them out. One day Grandma caught me and spanked me. I continued to hate avocados until long afterward, when my wife made guacamole dip.

Grandma pressed Mahoney to set up an appointment with Roach, but he returned empty-handed, muttering about Roach's busy schedule and how impossible it was to get to him. Undaunted, Grandma pushed Mahoney aside and took me by the hand to the Hal Roach Studio on Washington Boulevard in Culver City. She marched me directly into the casting office and announced that a talent scout in Dallas had promised a meeting with Mr. Roach.

Her imperious manner probably awed the casting director. He asked us to sit down while he would ask whether Mr. Roach could see me. Mr. Roach was able to see me — alone. That was how I met him in his office.

The casting director told Grandma that, since I was still very much a minor, my parents would have to sign a contract before a Superior Court judge in Los Angeles.

"Well, sir, you're going to have to wait on that. They're back in Dallas," Grandma told him.

"That's no problem, ma'am. We'll wait."

Talk about elation! I know I was elated, and you can take it to the bank that Grandma was, too. She got on the phone to Dallas, and eventually — long-distance meant *long*-distance in those days — she told my parents: "They've just offered Tommy a contract. And," she added, "you'll have to move to California. I'll wait here with him."

That meant my parents would have to sell their home, get my sister ready, and make plans to relocate. Getting Jane ready wasn't easy. She was in school where she had many friends. She was always a bit jealous of me. After years of preparing for the ballet, little brother had upstaged her. She had always been top banana. Now I was top banana. And I had done it with a mere song.

Our parents didn't let Jane's feelings stand in the way. Elation carried the day. When they decided to make the move, that was it. It was Dad who made the biggest sacrifice. Jane would enter a new school and make new friends, but Dad had a good job in Texas, and during the Depression people with jobs didn't leave them easily. To do so and expect to find work in California was chancy. Yet Dad did it. He was *that* kind of guy.

Dad, Mom, and Jane set out for Hollywood on the Southern Pacific's Sunset Limited. Grandma rented a house in

Culver City, closer to the studio, to prepare for their arrival. Culver City had only one hotel. Like most towns then, it still had street cars (most kids rode bikes to get around), and the streets were constantly being patched with tar to fill the cracks caused by frequent earthquakes. The Culver City house was a stopgap, temporary. We had taken a gamble in coming to Hollywood, and although we had won the first toss, we didn't know what to expect next. What lay ahead?

Studio Life

First there was the contract.
    When Mr. Roach hired me, the casting director told Grandma that the contract which my parents would sign would be a five-year deal. A five-year guarantee of employment in one of the best studios in Hollywood was a dream come true. Moreover, salaries for the *Gang* ranged from $50 to $600 a week. I was to be paid $50 at the start, with a raise to $60 after a year. That was a good salary for anyone in those days, and princely for an untried kid. After all, my dad had earned $40 as a commercial artist in Dallas, and we all lived comfortably on that. Remember, things were cheap then. For example, after we moved to California we bought an acre of ground with lots of trees in Encino for $900, and Dad built a house for $7,500. Grips and prop men at the studio earned $5 for a 12-hour day — but you could get a bowl of chili,

French fries, and a malted milk for fifteen cents. So in terms of those times I was very well paid.

But the deal was a contract with options. Two-sided options are O.K. I don't think anybody would object to them. However, the studio contract had options for only one of the two parties — and I'll let you guess which. "Said second party" [that's me], the contract stated, "will devote his entire time and attention to the services of the first party [that's Hal Roach] . . . The services shall be exclusive in all particulars. . . . "I could not engage in any outside work without permission of the studio. I couldn't quit. Yet the studio could fire me at any time on thirty days' notice. Even if it fired me, I granted "perpetual and exclusive right" to Hal Roach to use, sell, or license the use of my likeness. Finally, the studio could sell or transfer the contract to anyone else — any other movie or radio studio (or TV, when TV came in), any vaudeville or theater production — at any time "without any restrictions whatsoever."

So Mr. Roach owned me for five years. He could renew my contract annually, but I couldn't walk away.

Don't get me wrong. I'm not saying that Mr. Roach cheated me. My parents would have brought me to Hollywood for just $5 a week, options or not. I tend to think that, never having had anything to do with studio contracts, they were sure it was entirely fair, especially if the other kids were getting the same deal.

One of our two-reelers, *Our Gang Follies of 1938*, told it like it was. In that film one of the *Gang*, squeaky-voiced Alfalfa, imagines he has a great voice and decides he would rather sing for an opera company than for *Our Gang's* musical show. He pursues the impressario Barnaby (Henry Brandon, a character actor famous for evil or exotic roles) until the impressario humors him by giving him an opera contract, to take effect twenty years hence, when Alfalfa would be a grown singer.

After flaunting his contract among others of the *Gang*, Alfalfa takes a nap. He dreams that twenty years have passed and he is making his debut in *The Barber of Seville*. But the boos, hisses, and catcalls force the curtain down. Barnaby, holding Alfalfa to the contract, puts him out on the street with a tin cup to sing for pennies. Meanwhile, Spanky and the *Gang* also have grown up and have opened a swanky club. Alfalfa decides to swallow his pride and sing in Spanky's club, but Barnaby, using his option, tosses him back into the street. Alfalfa wakes up, but the one-sided option was no dream at Roach's or anywhere else in the movie capital.

In fairness to Mr. Roach, I must say that he had to have some protection in the case of unknowns. If a kid didn't cut it, he had to have a way to get rid of him. He wasn't running a charity or a halfway house for aspiring talent. He was running a business that had to make successful movies and make them fast — otherwise no profits. No profits, no studio. Still, the studio owned its people body and soul while they were under contract — and there was the perpetuity clause.

Anyway, the contract was signed, and Dad went back to close out his commercial art job and sell the house in Texas. It took him four or five months, during which time he batched it.

Meanwhile I got acquainted with the studio and the routine there. My first impression of the studio and the sets for *The Our Gang Comedies*, an impression that stayed with me, was of the dirt (remember my reaction to *Ben Hur*?). For the sake of realism Roach had an earth floor both inside the *Gang*'s "clubhouse" set and outside. A layer of earth up to a foot deep was laid on the stage. I had to get used to the dirt. I also had to get used to hollow buildings. The studio used lots of balsa for walls, false fronts, sometimes entire sets, and breakaway furniture. Often it was pre-cut to leave a realistic impression if the scene called for it to crash. It was harmless if it fell on you.

I was taken to the wardrobe and introduced: "This is Tommy." The wardrobe attendants looked me over. They didn't want to dress me like others others in *Our Gang*, They had their established images — Spanky with a beanie, Scotty in a baseball cap, and so on. The wardrobe people came up with the little shirt, suspenders, porkpie hat and baggy knickers that became part of my identity on the screen. As far as costume fittings were concerned, there weren't any. We wore hand-me-downs from the Salvation Army grab bag. The unwritten rule for *Our Gang* — and a lot of other comedies — was that if it didn't fit, it was right. Our clothes were baggy, our hair was long and shaggy, and makeup, with the sole exception of Alfalfa's Vaseline cowlick, was nonexistent.

I met Bob McGowan, Roach's director for *The Our Gang Comedies*. He was a retired Denver fireman who came to Hollywood, joined the Roach studio in 1921, and soon worked his way up. He acted indifferent toward me when we met and even afterwards (later I'll have more to tell about him and his attitude toward some of the various members of *Our Gang*). At the beginning I was the new kid on the block, an innocent amid pros. I couldn't tell the cameramen from the prop men, the key grip, the gaffer, the electrician, or any of the other guys behind the cameras. They were just a bunch of fellows who knew their jobs, put the thing together, and filmed it. I didn't know what I was supposed to do, and no one told me. McGowan's way of directing was simply to say, for example: "Kids, go over there. Now, Spanky, do this. . . . " Add to my ignorance the trauma of walking onto a set, having the lights turned on, and seeing that the houses were only fake fronts. I had to get used to all that and to performing. We might be told to look scared, but McGowan didn't direct except to say, "Look more scared." I was looking as scared as I could.

I may have been bewildered at first, but I had no stage fright. After all, I was only five-and-a-half, and you had to be a bit older, I think, to understand why you should feel stage fright. To a little Texas kid the lights, the cameras, the many people on the sound stage were all impressive — not frightening.

Gradually a day-to-day routine set in. My mother or grandmother drove me to the studio. I never took the red studio bus with the *The Our Gang Comedies* logo on its side. In fact, I didn't mix much with the other performers because we were all working on different projects at assorted sets on the lot. We filmed, we ate together with our mothers at the children's table in the studio commmissary (called the *Our Gang* Restaurant), we reported to our teacher in the studio schoolroom between takes, and we filmed again.

A guy remembers his first teacher. Mrs. Fern Carter was my first, and what a great teacher she was! The studio employed her to teach us, and she took the job seriously. She wore her hair in a tight bun, wore plain dresses, and was a strict disciplinarian. She wasn't indoctrinated with sensitivity training — no teacher was in those days — and we learned our lessons, or else! If you had told her about such things as developing self-esteem in pupils, she probably would have responded, "Let them do something to feel good about, and then they'll have self-esteem." Her voice was pleasant and her pronunciation precise. If she had a weakness, it was that she liked to talk, and having a group of *Gang* kids' mothers about, she had an audience. The mothers had to be at the studio with us by state law.

Our day at the studio ran from 8 a.m. to 5 p.m., with an hour off for lunch and three hours for schooling. That wasn't a straight three hours. It was broken up as the studio's needs dictated. The California Department of Education demanded that we spend a minimum of 180 minutes a day in class, and Mrs. Carter kept a log, recording the time we came to class, left to return to the set, came back, etc. If it looked as though the day was drawing to a close and we hadn't put in our 180 minutes, she told the director: "Quit shooting, they have to be in school." His response was always, "O.K., Mrs. Carter." She had the law on her side.

Our schoolroom was upstairs at the back of the studio office building, with regular school desks, but when all of us were needed on the set and were on call there, she worked with us at a utility folding table in a corner off the set. The table was screened off and far enough from the sound stage so the noise could not interfere. There she would go over our lessons with us.

Before becoming a teacher, Mrs. Carter had been in show business with her husband, so she understood the studio's needs, as well as our needs as children and as pupils. A wonderful lady — and so sociable. She knew our parents, and frequently visited our homes. Since our mothers were at the studio, Mrs. Carter would sit off the set with them, knitting and gossiping while we were performing. *Our Gang* included both white and black kids, and our mothers got along fine.

I believe we got a better primary education than many pupils in regular schools, because ours was intensive and mostly one-on-one. Mrs. Carter stuck to the three R's, using flash cards for addition, subtraction, multiplication, and division. In case you don't remember, one side of the card carried a problem, the other side the answer. I believe they still use these cards in school, so I guess they work. We went through English, history — all the required subjects. Because of our different ages, we were in different grades, but we had the advantage of a class ratio of, at most, one to twelve students, instead of one to thirty, as in so many schools. Mrs.

Carter taught only the principals (me, Spanky, Scotty, Darla, Stymie, etc.). A resource teacher who helped Mrs. Carter taught the other kids, and the extras went to their own schools when not working.

We had a close relationship with Mrs. Carter. She made sure that we had a Christmas tree and presents, and celebrated all the different holidays. When the *Gang* transferred to MGM in 1938, she went with us. It just wouldn't have been the same without her.

After I got acclimated I came to appreciate why the studio was called "the Lot of Fun." I remember Laurel and Hardy driving by in their trademark Model T, waving at us. Patsy Kelly and Thelma Todd were friends on and off the screen. Patsy was a wonderful girl and Thelma was just simply a love. Patsy played the wisecracking, hard-hearted type — Thelma the big-eyed, softer roles. Billy Gilbert, with whom I later worked in *Rosalie*, and ZaSu Pitts would notice us and spark our confidence with a "looks good!" Mr. Roach himself would come by sometimes and wave, with a hearty "Hi, kids! How's it going?" And he would do his little shtick, knowing we'd be pleased to see the big boss having fun, too.

If we didn't lunch at the studio commissary, we had lunch together at a little place across the street or took a box lunch out by the pretty goldfish pond that Roach put there for our pleasure. Sometimes we had birthday parties at our commissary table. The studio was a great place.

The best part was what it did for me. I knew I was a good actor, and now I found I was famous. Everyone knew *The Our Gang Comedies*. Whenever I joined the *Gang* in public appearances at places like a hospital for mobility-impaired children, or a Cocoanut Grove evening fund-raiser for underprivileged children, we'd be introduced as members of *Our Gang* from the Hal Roach Studios, and the audience would applaud enthusiastically in appreciation.

The studio receded into the background and family life took over after a day on the lot. We left by an alley and headed home, where family and friends were the focus. The family never went out of their way to see their star on the silver screen. Neither did the star himself. If we were at a Saturday matinee and an *Our Gang* feature came up on the screen, it was purely by chance that we were there. Some people can't understand that, but it's very simple. When you've worked on a film, week after week on a lot, the last thing you want to see is yourself in the theater on your days off.

Before Dad went back to Texas to close down his job and sell the house, he found a house for sale for us on Renfrew Road, near Sunset and Bundy, in Brentwood. Mom, Jane, Grandma, and I left the Culver City house and moved into the new home. After Dad came back he found work in his field in Los Angeles — easily, I might add, considering the Depression — and I became the second largest wage-earner in the family.

We settled into the red-tiled, Monterey-style house in Brentwood for several years. Brentwood was beyond Hollywood, past the Beverly Hills Hotel and Will Rogers Park, where the stars liked to play polo. We liked driving down Sunset Boulevard, which then had a bridle path down the middle. It led to the beach, and stars used the bridle path. The house was on a cul-de-sac called Tiger Tail Drive. It was located in a canyon with a stream running by. It stood on stilts between two houses, one above and one below. The natural setting was beautiful, and we had interesting neighbors.

There weren't many neighbors, but enough for us to have fun. Once or twice a year, as on Independence Day, we all got together and went to the beach for a block party. It may be hard to picture today, but Malibu was uncrowded, the ocean was clear, there were lots of starfish and urchins to be found on the shore. And there were no warning signs about pollution. There didn't have to be. Our parents set off fireworks, while we kids were allowed sparklers. We ate hot dogs and hamburgers and watched the *Rex* out at sea 'til the wee hours. The *Rex* was a gambling ship outside the three-mile limit. It was popular with actors, producers, and other swells.

Among our neighbors were the Wagners, John and Jane and their daughter Sarita. He was a test pilot for Lockheed. Down the street were Jane O'Brien and her brother Bill. Jane, who changed her name to Bryan, later became an actress and played opposite Bette Davis in *The Sisters* (Warner, 1938) and *The Old Maid* (WB, 1939). Bill, who dated my sister, died in action in World War II.

One thing I disliked about the Brentwood area — it swarmed with snakes. They crawled up into our house and they tried to eat the fish in our pond. Grandma killed them with a hoe.

Beautiful as the Brentwood natural setting was, with canyon, stream and all, it proved disastrous in the end. For one thing, the damp weather bothered my sinuses and my sister's too. Then in 1937 there were record-breaking rainfalls all over California. From the 1880s onward, many houses in the Los Angeles area were built in rocky washes. This was one of them. Swollen by the heavy rains, the stream that had flowed pleasantly on its way to the ocean suddenly became a raging river which rose into our home and left six inches of mud all over the beautiful floors. Dad got us out, and we had to live elsewhere for two weeks, but the charm of living in a canyon had faded. Then the doctor convinced my parents that the location was too cold and foggy for my nose and Jane's lungs. We had to move to the San Fernando Valley, where the climate was relatively dry and more healthy. We rented a small old frame house in Tarzana and looked for something better. We found it on Zelzah Avenue, on the Encino side of the Encino-Tarzana line. That was where Dad built the house for $7,500. It was California ranch style — stucco, with a long front porch.

In those days the San Fernando Valley was an agricultural area, given over to cattle grazing and orange groves. There were few houses. Clark Gable and Spencer Tracy had big spreads. Others of the movie colony were beginning to build there, but there really was little in the way of development. Then there were the Andersons. Mr. Anderson worked in aircraft while trying to raise millions of chickens scientifically. After he died of a heart attack, Mrs. Anderson got rid of the chicks. Other neighbors were the Olands, who were friends of Peter Lawford's family, and cousins of actor Warner Oland, the original Charlie Chan in the detective movies.

I enjoyed my boyhood there. I made model airplanes, the little balsa-wood ones, powered by rubber bands or gasoline engines. I loved to read — I think every actor does, because of the power of imagination. I had intended to continue in acting the rest of my life. I especially enjoyed the *Oz* books and collected all of them. I devoured comic books and what were called "Big Little Books," which were about three-by-four inches. I didn't have time for sports, unfortunately, until later. It was a laid-back community, similar to some San Joaquin Valley towns today, like Orange Cove, Kerman, and Dinuba.

I was eleven years old when we moved to the San Fernando Valley. I entered the Encino public school. There I competed in track, football, and tennis. I was easygoing and made friends quickly, once I had overcome the fellows who believed that any kid who acted was a sissy or who, on the contrary, disliked me because of the tough character I often played. There

31

were still some types who believed that what they saw on the screen was real life. I guess by fighting them I proved them right.

But here I am, running ahead of my story, and I haven't yet told about the other members of *Our Gang* and the films we made.

Child's Play

M̲r. Roach chose his youthful actors with an eye for a kid's face and personality. In a 1980 television interview he told my son that he had wanted "natural actors." That's why the *Gang* was so successful. He wasn't looking for the sweet Shirley Temple type. He wanted ordinary, innocently mischievous kids.

He started *Our Gang* after he saw some boys arguing and scrapping over sticks they had picked up in a lumber yard across the street from his office. "I want a bunch of kids like that," he told his casting director. They had to have individual character, and at the same time had to be recognizable types. The boys were little rascals. The females had the natural beauty of little girls with cherubic faces. On screen the innocent little boys vied for the attention and favor of the innocent little girls.

When I joined the group in 1932, *Our Gang* was firmly established as part of the Hollywood comedy scene. *Our Gang* shorts had already become standard screen fare back in the days of the silents. Mr. Roach released 88 silents in the series between November 1922 and November 1929. Audiences were familiar with "Sunshine Sammy" Morrison and other *Our Gang* members of that first period: Jackie Condon, Peggy Cartwright, Mary Kornman, Mickey Daniels, Jackie Davis, Allen "Farina" Hoskins, Joe Cobb, Jean Darling, and Mary Ann Jackson.

After the silents came three further distinct periods in the history of the *Gang*. The introduction of sound ushered in the second period, a series of twenty-three early talkies released between May 1929 and February 1932. Many of the original cast of the silents appeared in these first talkies, plus a few new actors, such as Matthew Beard, Dorothy De Borba, Bobby "Wheezer" Hutchins, and George "Spanky" McFarland.

Our Gang's golden era followed that batch of early talkies. This third period in the history of *Our Gang* comprised seventy-eight comedies made between March 1932, and May 1940. I joined the *Gang* in this, its heyday, and was featured in twenty-seven of those films. I played alongside Dorothy, Stymie, Spanky, Sid "Woim" Kibrick, Darla Hood, William "Buckwheat" Thomas, Gordon "Porky" Lee, and Carl "Alfalfa" Switzer. Mr. Roach sold the series to MGM in 1938, so some of the later films of this period were released under the MGM label.

There was a fourth period of MGM of *Our Gang* shorts, consisting of thirty issued between May 1940 and April 1944. The cast for these included some of the old-timers, such as Buckwheat, Darla and Alfalfa, and a lot of new kids — Billy "Froggy" Laughlin, Mickey Gubitosi (later renamed Robert Blake), Jackie Horner, and Janet Burston.

Child actors do not remain children forever, and conse-
quently there was inevitable turnover in the cast during the
twenty-two years the series lasted. But there was also a good
deal of carry-over from year to year and period to period. In
each period the leading figures were a pretty stable bunch,
and it took a while for a new member of the cast to move up
— while his or her time as a child actor was running out.

On the other hand, the director, who assigned the leading
roles, suffered no time limitation in his job. When I joined
the *Gang* Bob McGowan had been director for a full decade.
I've already mentioned his style of directing (or maybe I should
call it non-directing), as well as his indifference toward me. It
wasn't outright coldness, just cool. He simply ignored me, the
newcomer, and made me feel inferior. He concentrated on
favorites.

His prime favorite was George "Spanky" McFarland.
Spanky, like me, came from Dallas. He was two years younger.
He was modeling baby clothes and doing Dr. Pepper ads when
he was only three, and he joined the *Gang* at that early age.
This gave him more than a two-year lead over me at the studio. He was cute, and McGowan got him to do things others
couldn't — or just didn't — do. But Spanky won audience
favor, too, or McGowan wouldn't have pushed him up front as
he did.

How did they determine audience favorites? They held
previews and handed questionnaires to the viewers, asking
what they liked or didn't like and why. The survey responses
went to casting and from there to Roach himself. The public
liked Spanky. He became a money-maker, and McGowan probably thought Spanky was his meal ticket. It's a business, after
all. I didn't feel jealous of Spanky, but I disliked McGowan,
both for his non-directing and his indifference toward me.

Gus Meins replaced McGowan as director in March 1934,
when I had been part of *Our Gang* for two years. Meins, a

former newspaper cartoonist, was a scholarly looking man with horn-rimmed glasses. He was much quieter than the talkative and dynamic McGowan, and more relaxed with us kids. I don't know why they changed directors. One day McGowan was on the set, and the next day, there was Meins. We still didn't get much direction, however, and Meins, too, played favorites. However, he was not as open or as consistent regarding his favoritism, so it's hard for me to say now who his favorites were.

Did the kids' parents interfere? Mine never did. The players' mothers weren't pushy stage mothers, on the whole, but I'm pretty sure that some did interfere in ways that weren't too obvious. Certainly they wouldn't allow their kids to be upstaged, and they must have tried to exert some influence on Roach and the directors.

I don't blame parents who tried to get the best for their children. I especially empathize with the mothers of the extras who tried to speak up openly for their children — with good cause, but not always successfully. For them it wasn't just a question of getting a lead role or even a line or two, it was often a matter of keeping the extras from being badly treated. We principals had it easy, but the extras, though protected by studio teachers and social service workers, had a hard time. They were herded like cattle, had to provide their own wardrobes, and had none of the privileges of the regular *Our Gang*. In short, they were second-class citizens of the studio. It was among the principals, however, that favoritism prevailed.

Spanky was McGowan's invariable favorite. He was paired with Scotty Beckett, and the story generally revolved around these two "pals." I put "pals" in quotation marks because in real life the two actually detested one another. Once in school Spanky got so mad with Scotty that he jumped out of his seat and chased him down the runway to the first floor. Mrs. Carter was angry. "I won't have that kind of behavior here," she announced in the best teacher tone calculated to lay down the law.

Scotty was a pretty boy with big brown eyes. He left the *Gang* for a while and came back as Cousin Wilbur, a Waldo type. He was the scholarly, sheltered kind with horn-rimmed glasses, in contrast to us scuffy street urchins. He played in several other movies, and then we lost touch. In the forties he worked in such films as *The Jolson Story* (1947) and *A Date With Judy* (1948). He did some TV work in the early fifties, but his last ten years were filled with divorces, drug problems, and arrests. After suffering a beating, he checked into a Hollywood nursing home, where he died in 1968. The coroner did not rule on the specific cause of death. Some called it a suicide. Sad.

Dorothy De Borba was the *Gang* sweetheart before Darla. She was cute, with curls and an attractive face. She was hired because she did a great job of crying in MGM's *Men of the North* (1930), starring Gilbert Roland, when she was five. She starred in two dozen *Gang* shorts. Today she retains a tack-like sharpness and has a great outlook on life. Over the years Dorothy and I have agreed on a lot of things about the *Gang* days, but one thing on which we heartily disagree is Bob McGowan. She called him "Uncle Bob" and probably was one of his favorites, while I've already given my opinion of him.

Matthew "Stymie" Beard was already in the *Gang* when I joined. You may remember him as the little boy with the derby. Unfortunately, as an adult he developed a drug habit, but, much to his credit, managed to kick the habit. He worked with Synanon and later co-hosted a show with Jackie Taylor.

William "Buckwheat" Thomas started with a screen test at age three. He came after Stymie and was paired with Porky. Their whole dialogue was "otay." Since they were so young they could hardly speak lines or even pronounce "okay." Buckwheat was part of the Golden Era. His screen character always tried to side with Spanky and Alfalfa against Butch (me). He was a great kid. We were friendly, but we never became really close. Though we liked one another, our families didn't socialize. You see, my sister and I had many friends in and out of show business. Looking back, I'm glad we didn't confine ourselves to those in the business. As an adult, "Buckwheat" became a lab technician. In 1980 he told me he hadn't had as much fun in years as on the set of *Our Gang*.

Jackie Taylor, a long-legged little girl with a blonde pageboy haircut, was in only a few *Gang* shorts. Her best was probably *Hi'-Neighbor!* She made a career out of being an ex-*Gang* kid. She wrote a book about the *Gang, The Turned-On Hollywood Seven*. She hosted an *Our Gang* TV show in San Diego and Los Angeles, and even had a mail-order *Gang* fan club for a while. She was a bright and charming spokeswoman for the *Gang*.

Edith Fellows was slightly older than me and became a star by playing a little girl in Bing Crosby's *Pennies From Heaven* (1936). She came and went with the *Gang*, and our careers later merged and paralleled when we worked together in the *Five Little Peppers* series and with Leo Carrillo in *City Streets*.

Wally Albright was a *Gang* member when I started. He was curly blond, thin, and sickly looking. He played Waldo, a kid like himself. It was a straight part, not a character. Sometimes he sort of led the *Gang* with Spanky.

Tommy was my first role. Tommy was a nice, sympathetic character. (I became tough little Butch only later.) My debut was in *Spanky*, a two-reeler, with each reel lasting ten minutes. Like most of the shorts, each one took a week to shoot.

Almost a year of non-appearances followed, until March and April 1933, when *Forgotten Babies* and *The Kid from Borneo* were released. In *Forgotten Babies* Spanky baby-sits the *Gang's* younger brothers and sisters and ends up putting them in cages. In *Kid from Borneo* Spanky's uncle brings a wild man from Borneo to be his traveling side-show attraction. The wild man acquires a giant craving for candy and goes crazy every time he sees it.

I did little more than run around in these films. With non-direction and non-acting roles, I probably seemed to Mr. Roach to be a loser. But then came *Mush and Milk*. This was the first time McGowan gave me a prominent role, and it changed Roach's mind about me.

Mush and Milk, a two-reeler, was released in late May 1933. The story pits the kids against the nasty, scolding, old crone who runs the Bleak Hills Boarding School, a place right out of Dickens' worst nightmare. The title refers to the daily fare. The battle-ax's unfortunate husband is the teacher, an amiable gent, who calls on the kids for amateur entertainment during one class. When my turn comes after Stymie plays the harmonica, I step to the front of the class and belt out the torch song, "Just Friends (Lovers No More)." The adult lyrics ("We loved, we laughed, we cried, and suddenly love died . . . ") startle my classmates and teacher.

The song was popular in 1931, part of the repertoire of two crooners, Red McKenzie and Russ Colombo. Apparently Mr. Roach heard me at the piano with Marvin Hatley, the Roach studio composer. I was singing "Just Friends." He told Hatley, "Cute song . . . put it in the picture." I'm sure Roach spotted talent in me there and told McGowan to give me a break. Roach, after all, was head of the studio.

When it came to the filming, I sang the song impromptu, in a single take, without rehearsal or direction, and without a trace of stage fright. In the 1980 interview with my son, Edith Fellows remembered me as "braying like a coyote at the moon." But Leonard Maltin and Richard Bann, in their *Little Rascals* book, wrote of my performance that "this sequence is one of the most memorable in all *Our Gang* films — not the least because Tommy sings the song so earnestly and so well." So there, Edith. Add to this that *Mush and Milk* is my wife Polly's favorite of all my *Gang* shows.

Mush and Milk was the break I needed. And it didn't hurt one bit that Charley Chase, one of Hal Roach's adult comedy stars, saw me in it and told Roach, "I want that kid in one of my films."

Charley was an actor, director, and screen writer who had joined Roach in 1921. He specialized in characterizations of a dapper but bashful man-about-town whose meekness always got him into trouble with women. If he played a married man, he was the henpecked husband. He wanted a mean kid in his next one, and that's what he got with me in *I'll Take Vanilla*. In that film Charley's girl friend is my mom, a divorcée. She invites Charley to dinner and he brings the ice cream. She tries to force me to eat my spinach, and in the course of my refusal all kinds of high jinks ensue, such as flipping my spoonful into Charley's face.

That was the first time I played the tough "Butch" type, even though that was what Roach had hired me for. I never understood why Roach didn't use me that way from the start. Perhaps he wanted to let me get my feet wet and use me as a heavy in a year or so. It was a few years more before the Butch name and role were invented.

Charley was terrific, but so high strung that he reminded me of a thoroughbred horse. He was hyper, and worked best under pressure. And . . . he was great! He was very professional, loads of fun, and kind to all the cast and crew. I will always remember Charley Chase for building my self-esteem. He was the first director to guide me, to give me confidence and make me feel like somebody.

Between my success in *Mush and Milk* and Charley's *Vanilla*, it was a sure thing that Mr. Roach decided to keep me. McGowan and his successor, Gus Meins, had to use me. From September 1933 to September 1934, the studio issued eight *Our Gang* films, and I was in all of them (as Tommy).

The eight were *Bedtime Worries*, *Wild Poses*, *Hi'-Neighbor!*, *For Pete's Sake*, *The First Roundup*, *Honky Donkey*, *Mike Fright*, and *Washee Ironee*.

In *Bedtime Worries* Spanky sleeps alone for the first time and encounters a big-hearted break-and-entry burglar. Spanky thinks the burglar is Santa Claus. The *Gang* comes along, and the commotion wakes Papa and brings out the neighborhood cop. A wild mélée ensues.

Wild Poses deals with kids' antics when hauled before a photographer for a portrait session. In *Hi'-Neighbor!* a new snob on the block shows up with a shiny, pedal-propelled fire engine, and the *Gang* builds a wacky makeshift one of their own to compete with him. I volunteer to get the wheels, stealing them from baby carriages and bicycles.

For Pete's Sake gets the *Gang* into complications trying to obtain a doll for a sick little girl. *The First Roundup* is the story of the *Gang's* camping trip, during which Spanky and Scotty beat the others to the top of the hill by hitch-hiking. The camp-out at night inspires terror in the kids.

Honky Donkey features the kids' pet mule Algebra. Waldo, the rich kid, invites us rough types to his mansion. We take the mule along in his mother's chauffeured car, and the mule invades the mansion, bounding upstairs and into fancy rooms.

In *Mike Fright* I play a prominent part, getting the *Gang* into a radio audition. *Washee Ironee* has Waldo landing in a

41

mud puddle as he plays football with the *Gang*, just before he is supposed to give a violin recital for his mother's society friends. We try to help him wash his clothes, but they shrink. His mother sees us and calls the police, and her party turns into a shambles.

With the turn in my fortunes, I was launched. Thanks to my newfound confidence that Charley helped to inspire, I discovered that work (acting), came easy to me — easy as child's play. And child's play was our work. But a lot more than our acting went into creating the illusions and the comedy on the screen. Special effects, for instance . . .

World Of Illusion

One of the first things I had to get used to was that
the sets were so convincing, yet entirely unreal. *For
Pete's Sake*, for example, was shot on the "New York street"
backlot at Roach. The street included a store front, complete
with a dressed-up window — with nothing behind the front,
of course. Remember, Hollywood is a dream factory. When
we were filmed running down streets, it was on the back lot.
Outdoor scenes, too, were shot on the back lot. With exceptions like *Hi'-Neighbor*, Culver City was rarely used for a
setting. Even camping episodes were done in the studio. The
director and crew didn't like going on location, because out
there they lost control of lighting and sound. They used arc
lights on a catwalk to create the daylight image. What might
look like a forest, with sun shining through the trees, was
really a sound stage with arc lights. That was how we made

The First Roundup, which was the story of the *Gang*'s overnight camping trip.

Special effects — physical, visual, or auditory - are the dividing lines between film and reality. They create a mood, emphasize a point and, most importantly, make illusion convincing. They have been used in movies since Hollywood first started cranking out films. What with today's high-tech computer trickery, the public is so accustomed to special effects that they're just ho-hum, but in the old days they took some real ingenuity and they left audiences gaping.

Special effects fascinated me during my Texas childhood. When I came to the Roach studio I got a kick out of learning how effects were created in those days before modern technology changed everything. My own first professional exposure to special effects was with the *Gang* in *Hi'-Neighbor!* I was only six at the time. We filmed on a hill in Culver City. At most of our rare on-location shootings, the population was small and most of the residents were at work or in school. In *Hi'-Neighbor!* we build a crazy fire engine with the wheels that I swiped from bicycles and baby carriages. The fire engine careens down a hill at apparently breakneck speed. The seemingly wild, tumultuous ride didn't create much attention in the neighborhood — and there was a special reason. The truck was held by guide wires and the film was accelerated. Simple.

When I stole the wheels from bikes and baby carriages in the movie, I left the parent vehicles a bit crippled. Our film adventures never left the cast members in that condition. Despite every kind of mayhem on the screen, I can't remember anyone getting injured. There were all kinds of controls in every situation. But even with the best planning, bloopers occurred. The one that stands out in my memory happened in *Came the Brawn*, filmed when I returned to the *Gang* as Butch. I fell through the canvas of a boxing ring. Porky and

Buckwheat got mischievous and improvised — they pulled off my pants. I refused to come out until they gave them back to me. Talk about improvisation! We were on our own because the script, as usual, was lacking in detail. If what you ad-libbed made sense, the adults would allow it. Alfalfa had a terrible time memorizing lines, so he was the biggest improviser. The director generally said, "That's fine!"

Special effects produced a blooper of sorts when it came to Pete the Pup. Pete, the white dog that accompanied *Our Gang* as an actor in our films, was the longest-lived character in the series. There was a Pete with the *Gang* from its earliest silent days. The series outlived the original Pete, as he had three successors — four generations in all, you might say, although the dogs were not related. The original Pete was born with a half circle around his left eye. I was told by Gorden "Porky" Lee at a November 1993 meeting that Roach hired an unknown makeup artist to complete the circle. The artist was Max Factor! The later Petes had to have the full circle painted on by applying a liquid dye. But when one Pete passed on and a successor was found to take his place, the makeup staff sometimes didn't remember which eye was supposed to bear the familiar circle of black. Pete often appeared on the screen with a ring around the wrong eye. And then there was the time Pete played too long under the studio lights and had to be nursed through a siege of "Klieg eye."

When I was Butch, a scene was filmed in which the kids pelted the Woim and me with tomatoes. Try throwing a tomato at the wall, and you'll get only a watery-looking mess with just a hint of red. They filled the tomatoes with ketchup. The tomatoes went splat, and left a dark stain (and how they stank!).

Mike Fright, in which the *Gang's* "International Silver String Submarine Band" auditions on a radio show, had a scene where the racket we make with our little band causes the acoustic equipment to pop and the sound man's hair to stand on end. Bert Gordon played the sound man. It didn't require electricity to make his hair fly up, just brushing back his fine, long thatch in stop-frame. (Bert later played the Mad Russian on Eddie Cantor's radio show.)

Fishy Tales had several special effects. Alfalfa fires a suction-cup dart at Buckwheat, but hits me. The illusion was optically contrived. Alf shot the dart off-camera, a cartoon animation was used, and the dart was rigged to stick to my head. When the Woim and I chased Alf and Spanky through a barn door, the door was balsa wood, pre-cut to their figures so as to give way.

In *Kid Millions* I learned a formula for ice cream substitute. Eddie Cantor made this film for Sam Goldwyn in 1934. He used Stymie, me, and a couple of others from the *Gang*, although we didn't play as *Our Gang*. The last scene was set in an ice cream factory where a millionaire wanted to give poor, deprived kids all the sweets they coveted. Thousands of kids were seated at ice cream counters while an ice cream truck drove down the center aisle, dispensing mounds of the stuff. There was a problem of meltdown of the ice cream. It had to be eaten. The action couldn't be faked. The solution? A disgusting concoction of mashed potatoes and cheese. As featured actors, we lucked out and got the real thing, but the extras ended up with mashed potatoes and cheese — and they had to look pleased. Illusion, all right.

I saw a lot of special effects, and learned how they were created by watching the takes for the day, which are called "dailies" or "rushes." Mr. Roach sometimes came by to see them, too. They were interesting for anyone in the film industry. They were grainy working prints of the film, not a finished product. The clap board would snap, then the establishing shot would come on. This is a full shot at the beginning of a sequence which establishes the location, setting, and mood. There would be several more, then a two-shot, which is a close shot just wide enough to keep two people within the frame. After that, the over-the-shoulder shots would come up, and finally the closeups. Lines would be fed off-camera, and the actors would have to react to them. The dialogue director would feed cue lines, such as "What are you doing today, Tommy?" and my response, delivered while looking sideways at the camera, might be, "I'm going out in the back yard and dig for some worms."

There was one aspect of the Hollywood illusion business I didn't discover until later: Scandals had to be hushed up and the illusion of propriety maintained. I was only nine when Thelma Todd was murdered. The newspapers said she died "under mysterious circumstances." One theory was that she was murdered by the Luciano mob. Whenever we found out about Hollywood hanky-panky, we saw that it was kept quiet. If it came to light it could cause problems. A scandal involving Fatty Arbuckle resulted in his censorship by Hollywood. It also ruined Arbuckle's career. When Lee Tracy was drunk and urinated from a balcony on a Mexican general seated below, his career went with that flow. Scandals reflected not only on the actors, but on the studio and its profits.

Speaking of Thelma Todd and her partner, Patsy Kelly, I can't resist mentioning a small incident that occurred when they were making a movie at the same time as the *Gang*, on a sound stage next to ours. I ran into them daily. One day, while I was acting in a *Gang* feature, an assistant director from next door came looking for extras. He went up to my mother and grandmother. "Would you ladies like a job?" he asked. We've got a big theater set and we need some extras to play audience. Would you come in and sit in the audience? We'll pay you." So my mother and grandmother filled two audience seats in the Kelly-Todd stage comedy while we made our *Gang* movie.

Extras had a hard time during the Great Depression. So did unemployed crew. Mr. Roach treated his workers like family. He kept employees for twenty or thirty years. You saw the same electricians, prop men, special effects men, and cameramen. They were pros who knew what they were doing. They had been doing it for years and years. Roach trusted them and kept them through good times and bad. Only if he couldn't trust their work would he let them go.

In the Depression there were many whom other studios let go. I used to see them waiting outside our studio, just like extras, waiting for any work that day. There was no feeling among them of "We're in this together." Rather, it was highly competitive. Grips, prop men, electricians stood around until the assistant director might come out and say, "OK, I need ten prop men and fifteen grips." They would hold up their hands and he'd pick the ones he wanted. He had a pocket full of $5 bills, and as each man went in for a 12-hour day he'd be given a $5 bill.

Besides the film crews, there were also auxiliary workers at the studio lot, such as the still photographers, Stax "Clarence" Graves and his brother Bud "Chester" Graves. Stax was the official photographer for the Hal Roach studio, while Bud worked independently out of a studio in Culver City. They were pioneers in the business even though they didn't boast any great equipment, just flash bulbs and Graflexes, those big, hooded, upside-down box cameras. They stood you in an alcove in the stills lab for publicity photos. When we were shooting a scene, Stax would come right on the stage to photograph us. All of the publicity shots were processed in his studio right on the lot. The Graves were great to work with. They managed to photograph us even though we could be a pain to anyone who wanted us to sit still for any length of time. Stax was kindly, quiet, and so serious about his work that it left him open to all sorts of pranks. We were quite a challenge, making faces, punching, pulling, and scratching. Yet he had a way of getting us to cooperate. Stax shot all of Roach's comedians — the *Gang*, Patsy Kelly, Laurel and Hardy, and Charley Chase.

Bud was a wonderful man. When Grandma and I arrived in Hollywood and lived in the boarding house, he befriended us and drove us all around southern California each Sunday afternoon. Bud made many of my publicity stills and you'll find some of them in this book.

While I was becoming part of this great bunch of actors and film makers, things kept changing, including directors' favorites. First, there was the established favorite, Spanky. Then Alfalfa started to get bigger parts, and eventually he became the main character with Spanky as his sidekick. Then *Mush and Milk*, plus Charley Chase's interest in me, brought me forward. In the end, director Meins began bringing in new kids and he phased me out. My contract was terminated. My parents and I were not that troubled. My world didn't change.

I didn't know I would be returning to *Our Gang* eventually.

Into Radio

My world really didn't change because I was pretty young and resilient. I remember my mother assuring me that although I wouldn't be working at the Roach lot I'd be doing other things. It wasn't all that hard, leaving Roach and the *Gang*. It brought a feeling of coming to the end of a term, and an expectation that I would go on to something else. My mother's attitude carried over to me; it could be summed up as: "Well, there are other things in Hollywood besides the Hal Roach studio."

Dad was working, and since I was not the sole support there was never any pressure to get another acting job. I believe that, had I chosen to sit out the next five years, my parents and grandmother wouldn't have batted a collective eye.

I had already been attending Encino public school. My

sole problem there was acceptance. My classmates were farm kids and real estate promoters' kids — no actors' kids. Everyone has a cross to bear, a man of the cloth once told me. Mine was borne in the first week at Encino school, where I got into ten fights in five days. As I mentioned earlier, I was recognized, and the fellows would say, "Aw, you're one of those sissy movie kids." I had to prove myself, day in and day out, in battle after battle. I got tired of this after a week — and who wouldn't? One day Bob Reed, one of the schoolyard leaders, came up to the school bully and said, "Leave him alone. He's trying to be like everyone else." The bully responded: "No way. I'm gonna beat him silly." Young Reed: "You'll have to fight me first." The bullying stopped.

Bob Reed was an ordinary kid, and we became good friends. His father owned a real estate office, "Bob's Good Earth," and he sold to actors moving out to Encino and Tarzana. Bob taught me to play football, which I had played only in movies, and taught me other sports as well. I loved it, and became just like everyone else in that gang — a real gang. They were a tough bunch to know, because they didn't want anything to do with show-biz kids.

I stayed in show biz after I left *Our Gang* — I just went on to do other things. In the late thirties Warner Brothers used my voice as that of a little devil (naturally), an angel, a parrot, Peter Rabbit and other characters in several *Merry Melodies* cartoons. George Fleishman created *Merry Melodies*, which evolved from the original *Looney Tunes*. They were devised in order to make use of the music Warner Brothers had bought. Each cartoon had to use a Warner *Looney Tune* song, regardless of whether it fit the plot.

I remember one of the times I played a little devil. The cartoon was entitled *Don't Look Now*. The story concerned two dogs that wanted to marry, an angel who tried to unite them, and me, the devil who wanted to break them up. But wait! I was also the voice of the little angel, Dan Cupid.

Between 1935 and 1938, I was Buddy in *Mister and Missus Is the Name*, Peter Rabbit in *My Green Fedora*, a baby scarecrow in *I'd Love to Take Orders from You*, Owl Jolson in *I Love to Sing*, Petey Parrot in *I Wanna Be a Sailor*, and a Freddy Bartholomew character in *The Major Lied 'Til Dawn*.

In *Mister and Missus*, a mermaid gets together with a merman. *Fedora* was re-used in *Toy Town Hall*, in which the cartoon becomes a little boy's dream. In *Sailor* the young parrot wants to follow in his father's footsteps and go to sea despite his mother's objections. *The Major Lied* has a British big game hunter telling a boy about his exploits in Africa.

Voice work in cartoons prepared me for radio. In radio, as in the movies, you work in the presence of others, but in my cartoons I never met the other performers. I'm sorry that I didn't meet the great voices of the cartoon world — Mel Blanc, the man of a thousand voices; Ben Benaderet, who was often Warner's voices, or the directors Ted Avery, Chuck Jones, and Friz Freleng. I was out of cartoons before I was old enough to appreciate who those people were.

The acting colony liked southern California for its climate, not its geology. When the Long Beach earthquake occurred in 1933, W. C. Fields was on a sound stage. He led his co-performers off the set as everything started to jitterbug. Our family was away on a two-week vacation in Texas. My parents remembered hearing about the great San Francisco quake of 1906, and we were sure that back in Los Angeles nothing was left. Returning, we saw cracked pavements, felt aftershocks, and found things generally jittery. The aftershocks worried actors, who felt uneasy on sound stages with big lights hanging overhead.

Our roots were now in Hollywood, and my parents were well established there, so they decided I should pursue a movie career. Please note that my mother was not a stage mother — not the pushing kind. Do you remember the scene in the *Our Gang Mike Fright* in which "Little Leonard" Kibrick's stage mother encourages him to play his trumpet even though the sight of me eating lemons causes his mouth to pucker uncontrollably?

My family got me an agent, Jack Sherrill. Jack was a typical agent, fast-talking and go-getting, but, unlike many, he wasn't a flesh peddler. He did not carry competitors simultaneously. He was entirely ethical.

An agent's earnings depended on the actor, so things moved. I played the mean kid in many Andy Clyde films, including *Alimony Aches* (1935), *Knee Action* (1937), and *Now It Can Be Sold* (1939). I also played the mean kid or Monty's kid in Monty Collins-Tom Kennedy two-reel comedies. I never had to audition for these roles. The studio called my agent, and I'd be sent in to talk to them. Someone in charge would take a quick look at me and pipe up, "Hi, Tommy! You want to make this movie? Send in your agent." And Tommy Bond's name would be in the credits. It didn't hurt on a resume.

Andy Clyde played at Columbia, and Monty Collins and Tom Kennedy were teamed at the same studio, making their comedy series. Monty was weasel-faced, skinny, beady-eyed and very funny. He played the nervous, henpecked, short-fused guy. Tom was noted for a gravelly voice, stocky build, and broken nose. He played dumb gangsters or prizefighters. Collins and Kennedy were paired to rival Laurel and Hardy, another team of smartie and dumb guy, but they were never really in the same league.

As for Andy Clyde, he never looked young, I guess. He was one of those ageless people who appear old forever. He played Walter Brennan types, "born old." Usually he played a loveable old hick — shy, "everyone's grandpa." Actually, he was just that kind of person — kindly and with a fine sense of humor. There is a publicity shot of him that was used in the newspapers. It shows him helping me with school work, not an uncharacteristic scene. Unfortunately, I lost contact with him after I left the Clyde comedies. Even now, half a century later, I regret that. But I don't regret what came next — radio.

Mr. Marconi's invention entered its prime about the time I was born. It became a major source of family entertainment. Warner Brothers had a lot on Sunset Boulevard in Hollywood, across the street from where KTTV is today, near KTLA and KMPC. All the classic early Warner pictures, such as *The Jazz Singer* and *Public Enemy*, were filmed on that lot. Warner Brothers had a radio station, KFWB, and a water tower with the sign "Warner's Vitaphone" on the lot. When a new program, Gus Edwards' *School Days of the Air*, was announced, thousands of kids came to try out for a part in this new radio show.

Gus Edwards was a legendary theater figure whose *School Days* sketches had been responsible for the discovery of Eddie Cantor, George Jessel, Walter Winchell and Lila Lee back in the 1910s. Early in the century he penned songs such as "By the Light of the Silvery Moon," "In My Merry Oldsmobile," "Jimmy Valentine," and "School Days." In the twenties and thirties he discovered many fine actors, including Eleanor Powell and Ray Bolger.

Gus Edwards was looking for all types of talented kids to be part of the radio show, on which he was going to be the host and Marian Mansfield was to fill the role of teacher. They were looking for a junior emcee, among other parts. Cantor, who had his own radio show with Bobby Breen, his protégé, movie co-star, and junior emcee, was one of the judges winnowing the candidates. He was there to advise Gus in the selection process.

I went to a cattle call where hundreds, thousands, millions of us auditioned and a dozen would be picked. I'm exaggerating, but not by much. The audition was held on the Vitaphone lot. There was a platform for the judges that faced thousands of occupied folding chairs.

Some of the kids were immediately let go with the standard "Don't call us, we'll call you — maybe the second Wednesday of next week." Hours later I was still waiting with others. I was picked, along with a boy pianist, a girl violinist, an accordion team and Sidney Miller, a friend of Mickey Rooney. The accordion team consisted of Milton DeLugg, Johnny Carson's orchestra leader for a short time, and Marshall, billed with him as Milton and Marshall.

What about me? Well, they needed a tough kid to ask the questions for the quiz show, to tell the jokes, and to sing. They needed a junior emcee, and that's where Mr. Cantor came in. He picked me for junior emcee, second banana on the show. I was to be the kid heckler, a first-class brat. (My job on *School Days of the Air* may have helped prepare me for the tough-kid role I was to have later when I returned to *Our Gang.*)

I needed voice coaching to be on radio. I had two coaches, Andre de Sigarola, who had been Deanna Durbin's teacher, and Johnny Marvin, a composer of Western songs.

If you've been in a radio studio in the past thirty years you can't possibly imagine the studios of half a century ago. They were huge. They could accommodate a full 32-piece orchestra and an audience of 350. Go to a radio station today, and what do you see? Cubbyholes.

One big difference between radio and movie studios in those days was that in radio you stood by the mike before an audience, script in hand. The audience was a vital part of the show. If one of Jack Benny's or Fred Allen's jokes died, it died. No canned laughter. After a joke was delivered, Benny would make a silent facial expression bound to get a reaction from the audience. This was essential to keep audience input alive. The audience made radio acting something like theater, except for the luxury of a script in hand.

Acting in "real time" before an audience on a network show was more unnerving than acting in front of a camera, where you had the option of retakes. There were no retakes in radio then. If you flubbed a line, you flubbed it in front of the whole nation.

Bert Fisk was our orchestra conductor. The show gave me a great opportunity to meet and work with the big names in old-time radio, and some who carried over to television — stars like George Burns and Gracie Allen, Milton Berle, Joe Penner, Joe E. Brown, and Edward Everett Horton. That was the caliber of guests we had on the show, many of them stars who owed their start to Gus. They reciprocated by having us as guests on their shows.

I loved it. And why not? How many nine-year-olds got to ride a limousine from work site to work site? Sometimes I was tied up on a movie shot and couldn't make all of the radio script meetings. That's where the writers went over the lines and gags with us and we rehearsed. I'd be picked up and taken to the studio by limo, going over the lines on the ride over.

Rehearsals were held in the afternoon, and the show went on in the evening. As in the films, the rehearsals were not necessarily in sequence. We might go over the opening, the introduction to the show, and then stop; rehearse individual numbers separately, then the lead-ins, and then the gags. When we performed before the audience, cues came from a director in the control room. He pointed at you, and that meant GO. In radio, directors were more like technicians.

Gus ran the show. He usually led off by singing some of his own songs, such as "By the Light of the Silvery Moon," one of those pre-World War I compositions that rhymed sentimental words. Then the show was back to the present and the age of the modern know-it-all brat. I kept the script to the side, using it only to refer to now and again, and when a gag came I'd put the script down and wait for the laughs.

We must have done A-OK, because we went big time. When the show began, KFWB was strictly local, for California consumption only. California didn't have the leading position in the nation that it holds today. After thirteen weeks on the air, however, CBS decided to pick us up. CBS didn't operate as a charity, so it must have seen something in our show — the old ratings boost. We went national, and Gus Edwards, already famous as "the star maker," began to enjoy a big budget. Thanks to our big sponsor, White King soap, big-name stars were brought on our show.

Eddie Cantor's radio show aired at a different hour. He felt a loyalty to Edwards for having discovered him, but they were nevertheless competitors. Friendly competitors. Bobby Breen, on Cantor's show, was a boy soprano with a nasal, high-pitched voice. I was also a soprano, and I used to sing a song each week on the show. Once I told Mr. Edwards that I could imitate Bobby Breen.

Edwards, skeptically: "You can? Let's hear you."

I held my nose and started to sing "Rainbow on the River," which Breen had made famous.

Edwards, convinced: "My God, it's Bobby Breen!"

I beamed, and he went on: "Why don't you do it on the show? We'll really fool Cantor!"

We got Bobby's own arrangement. The orchestra leader was alerted, and we went on the air. Mr. Edwards announced: "And now we're going to have a special song from a special guest."

When the director pointed to me I began to sing "Rainbow on the River." The audience roared with laughter.

Cantor was at home, listening. He was flabbergasted. He couldn't understand what had happened. He got right on the telephone to demand of Gus what Bobby was doing on our show.

Edwards, triumphantly: "That isn't Bobby Breen. That's Tommy, holding his nose."

Cantor reacted with an explosive laugh.

Gag feuds like that were typical among radio personalities. Jack Benny had one with Fred Allen. They were really friends, but folks at home heard all their bickering. Whether or not they believed them, they at least enjoyed them because ratings soared.

When we went national we had to employ electrical transcription. The station used a large (sixteen-inch) record which played at sixteen r.p.m. (do you remember that setting on those old phonographs?) to record the show for the three different time zones between L.A. and New York. Prime time, of course, was 7 p.m. to 10 p.m. We put on a show at 5 p.m. in Los Angeles, which was 8 p.m. in New York, and fed it by telephone lines to East Coast stations. Three hours later, 8 p.m. on the West Coast, the cast did a repeat show. Transcriptions and copies were made for stations that couldn't be reached because of the time difference. A copy was kept for use as a substitute in case anyone fell ill at a scheduled show time. This was to be used only in emergencies, for until 1946, when Bing Crosby broke the ban, the networks had a general rule of no canned shows.

Gus Edwards was a real gentleman. I can't say enough

about him and his lovely wife. When I first knew him, he was in his seventies. His voice was a bit shaky, but he was still able to sing. He had a large build, white hair, and the biggest brown eyes. They could command respect with a glance. He was quiet, patient, a calming influence on the show and very much in control. Sometimes, surprisingly, he would become nervous, and I would have to emcee the show to take a load off him. I remember his wife as a charming lady who sat in the sponsors' booth while the show was going on.

Harry Maizlish, the KFWB general manager, was another true gentleman. He was like a second father in many ways. He was mighty close with a dollar, but big-hearted. He looked more like a doctor than someone in show biz, not that they have a particular look that I can define. He was tall, with wavy black hair, glasses and a clean-shaven face. Neither an introvert (a no-no in show biz) nor a marked extrovert, he was always amiable, kind and appreciative of the job I did on the show.

Through Mr. Maizlish I met absolutely fantastic people, all friends of his. On May, 6, 1937, I made my first visit to San Francisco by train, accompanied by Mr. Maizlish. I was eleven years old. I remember the date because when we arrived, the news of the *Hindenburg* disaster came over the radio station teletype.

We were dinner guests of M. and Mme. Paul Verdier at their penthouse. M. Verdier owned the old City of Paris department store that his grandfather Felix had founded during the Gold Rush. Julia Altrocchi, historian of old San Francisco society, described the Verdiers in her *Spectacular San Franciscans* (Dutton, 1949) as "conspicuously identified with modern San Francisco and with many an admirable enterprise on behalf of French and American welfare." But I identify them with elegance and chocolate. Mme. Verdier came to dinner in an evening gown. She gave me bitter Parisian chocolates. I kept the box for many years, until it was destroyed in a fire of which I shall speak later.

Through Mr. Maizlish I also met George Jessel and his wife, Norma Talmadge, together with Marion Davies (William Randolph Hearst's mistress). Never was a meeting so easily arranged. "Would you like to go to the Jessels' house?" Harry asked one morning.

"Sure," I responded.

"Well, let's go."

The Jessels lived near the Miramar Hotel in Malibu, and Miss Davies was their neighbor. Mr. Jessel, in an ornate smoking jacket, complete with ascot, asked me: "How would you like a good Jewish breakfast?" I was stumped. In my eleven years I had never heard of a Jewish breakfast. While I was wondering what it was, he said: "Oh, here she is now!"

"She" was his wife. Norma Talmadge descended the stairway in a silk dressing gown, with a train to the floor. She was lovely, and when I later found out who she was and what she had been in the old days, I was properly impressed. Anyway, I'll never forget that dressing gown. I *was* impressed. The breakfast was great, too — matzoh bread, unsalted butter, cheeze blintzes. Marion Davies came over later that morning for a visit, and that's how I chanced to meet her.

I wasn't star struck. I felt a part of the business, and I knew these were just other human beings who put their trousers on one leg at a time, like everyone else in the world. But these people *were* legends. I'd seen them in the movies.

Another thing about Harry. After each show he took me to the Brown Derby, or sometimes to Schwab's Drugstore, where Lana Turner and others were discovered. There were two Brown Derbys in Hollywood — the tourist trap shaped like a derby on Wilshire, and the one on Vine Street where the Hollywood crowd went. There the waiters concocted dinner before your eyes (including flambéed cherries jubilee), and practically stood on their heads to satisfy their patrons. No cheap tastes here! My favorite was filet mignon. There we were, my mother, Harry, Gus and his wife, the guest star, and me. A far cry from Texas!

The Brown Derby had brown leather booths. The walls were lined with caricatures of all the movie stars, drawn by a man who came to your table to sketch you. As you entered, there was a bar at the side and the dining room straight ahead. The bar was placed so that anyone there could see everyone coming in. The Derby was informal, more like a club than a restaurant, and the actors and actresses delighted in it. Everybody knew everybody. Here they could and did let their hair down, and here real business was conducted.

I remember seeing Jack Oakie at the bar. Then he'd come over to our table and give me Sen-Sen breath sweeteners. He knew me from the radio show and from *Our Gang*. He always said how much he liked both. I never worked with him, but of course I knew him.

Others, too, table hopped. Here was a truly happy time with happy, fun-loving people, long before there were such things as "happy hours." I have to thank Harry for that experience.

During my two years with KFWB, San Diego held what it liked to call a World's Fair. My agent, Jack Sherrill, arranged to fly my mother and me down there so I could be crowned Candy King in a tie-in with the makers of Baby Ruth candy bars. Probably I was chosen because of playing children's roles in both radio and movies. It was my mother's first flight, and in a Piper Cub, at that. Was she scared! I crowned a little girl Candy Queen and flew back.

I was radio's fair-haired boy and, thanks to Mr. Maizlish's contacts with producers and others in the business, I made guest appearances on other radio shows. One that still sticks in my mind was an appearance on Milton Berle's "Gillette Community Sings." Berle had an ego larger than the iceberg that sank the *Titanic*. He didn't like being upstaged. I had a script with quite a few gags, but Uncle Miltie told the writers to scratch out whatever gags they had put in for me. Now, Mr. Maizlish hadn't loaned me to play patty-cake, so when I found out about the cuts I was ready to blow a fuse. I re-entered all the scratch-outs from the original script.

Miltie was so mad he could have bit nails. I had sand-bagged him. But I got the laughs, and after the show he shook my hand and gave me his ultimate expression of admiration. "Congratulations," he said. "You're a real pro. You did it to me, didn't you?"

That's the way it was in Hollywood. You had to have guts to survive, let alone make it. Guts helped me land the Butch role when I went back to the *Gang*.

I also worked on radio with George Burns and Gracie Allen, Joe Penner, Bert Lahr, Edward Everett Horton, and Joe E. Brown. In many cases I played their son. The work became easy after a while. Radio, after all, was radio, and one show was much like any other — go to a script conference, rehearse, and do it.

Mr. Maizlish did many good things for me. Thanks to the sponsor, I had a lot of fringe benefits — good exposure, good publicity — and I received new bikes, cameras, and projectors. Once I received a solid gold watch. But I was being paid only $25 a week. I was doing one or two numbers and helping Gus Edwards carry a national show with dialogue, while the other kids (with the exception of Sid Miller) had only to do one number and no dialogue. My agent, who wasn't getting a percentage of the bikes and watches, told me and my parents that I was underpaid. He tried negotiating with Mr. Maizlish, but Mr. Maizlish wouldn't budge. Maybe they weren't budgeted to pay more, though they had a good sponsor. The laborer is worth his hire, says the New Testament, so I left.

Sid Miller tried to fill the void, but the audiences wouldn't have it. The show was cancelled six weeks later. The public doesn't accept a new character in place of an established one. We've seen that in good shows and poor ones; people want a certain character. Take away that character, and the show isn't the same.

I saw Mr. Maizlish about fifteen years after that, when I was at KTTV and had to go over to KFWB on business. He was still the general manager. He was bitter about my leaving and the resultant demise of the show.

6

Back To The Gang

Anna May Wong was one of the very few Asian stars of early Hollywood, and one of the most photographed actresses of the thirties. Born in L.A.'s Chinatown in 1907, she started as an extra at age twelve and became a sensation in Douglas Fairbanks' *Thief of Bagdad* in 1924. When I was nine I played alongside Anna May Wong in one of Oliver Hinsdale's stage productions.

Hinsdale, a distinguished, elderly man, showcased actors' and actresses' talents at his theater in Beverly Hills. The Hollywood producers frequented his playhouse to see what they might turn up. I wanted stage experience and I got it there. There was no salary, but the experience and the exposure were invaluable.

Anna May Wong usually played the part of a seductive siren, but when I was with her in *The Sweetmeat Game* she

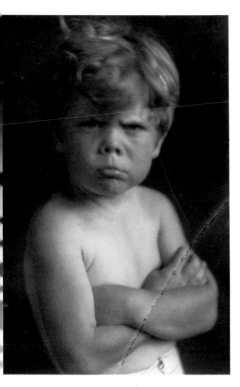

Grandmom Janie Sauter, 1932. Ready to take on Hollywood.

Tommy at age five, 1931.

Tommy's sister Jane Bond, 1941.

Tommy's parents Ashley and Margaret Bond, 1969.

Tommy at age eleven—the Junior Master of Ceremonies of *Gus Edwards' School Days of the Air,* 1937.

Graduation day at Van Nuys High School, 1945.   Tommy in the Navy, 1945.

A Valentine from *The Little Rascals*. Dickie Moore, Matthew "Stymie" Beard, George "Spanky" McFarland, Pete the Pup, Dorothy "Echo" DeBorba, Tommy, and Tommy McFarland. Courtesy King World Productions, Inc.

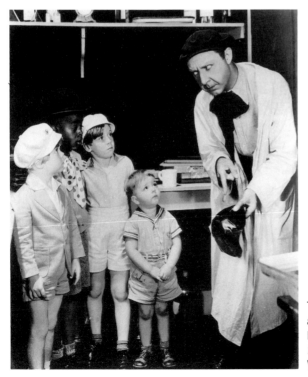

Tommy, Stymie, Jerry Tucker, and Spanky with Franklin Pangborn in a scene from *Wild Poses*, 1933. Courtesy King World Productions, Inc.

Hail, hail, the *Gang's* all here. Stymie, Wally Albright, Jerry Tucker, Jackie Taylor, Tommy, Donald Proffitt, Scotty, Spanky, and Pete. 1933. Courtesy King World Productions, Inc.

Tommy sneezes to get the donkey to pull the wagon in *Honkey Donkey*. Fillbrook Lyons, Stymie, Scotty, and Spanky look on. Courtesy King World Productions, Inc.

Stymie, Tommy, and Wally are scared of the dark in *The First Round-up*, 1933. Courtesy King World Productions, Inc.

Camping in the woods in *The First Round-up*, 1933. Courtesy King World Productions, Inc.

Everyone loves Pete in *For Pete's Sake*, 1933. Courtesy King World Productions, Inc.

For Pete's Sake, 1933. Jackie, Wally, Stymie, and Tommy look at Marianne Edwards holding the doll that was traded for Pete. Courtesy King World Productions, Inc.

A family portrait. Tommy, Emerson Treacy, Gay Seabrook, Bob Mc Gowen, Spanky, a friend, and Stymie. Courtesy King World Productions, Inc.

Having fun off the set. Tommy, Scotty, Spanky, and Stymie. Courtesy King World Productions, Inc.

Going to school on the Roach lot. Teacher Fern Carter, Tommy, Stymie, Spanky and friend. Courtesy King World Productions, Inc.

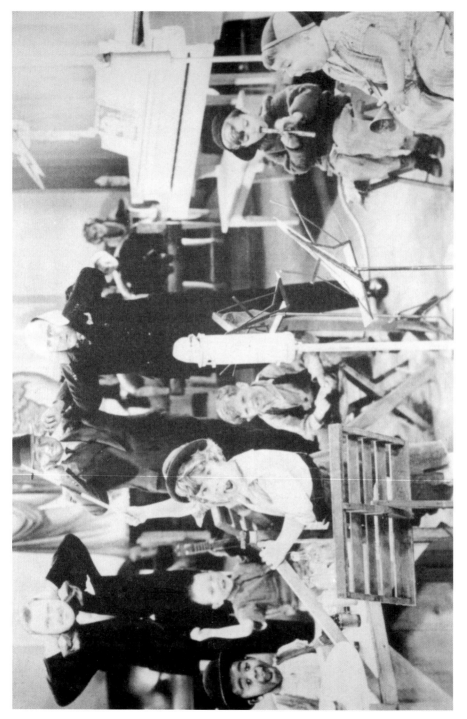

Mike Fright, 1933. Tommy leades the International Silver String Submarine Band. Courtesy King World Productions, Inc.

Glove Taps, 1936. Carl "Alfalfa" Switzer and Butch battle it out as Spanky referees. Courtesy King World Productions, Inc.

Washing Wally's clothes in *Washee Ironee*, 1933. Yen Wong, Tommy, Spanky, Leonard Kibrick, Jerry Tucker, and Stymie. Courtesy King World Productions, Inc.

The Gang with teacher Fern Carter driving the best home-made fire engine in the world in *Hi'-Neighbor!*, 1934. Courtesy King World Productions, Inc.

Nobody likes a tomato in the face! Sidney "The Woim" Kibrick and Butch, 1937. Courtesy King World Productions, Inc.

You're darn right it's Butch! Courtesy King World Productions, Inc.

Butch and Woim are taking good care of Alfalfa and Spanky, 1937. Courtesy King World Productions, Inc.

had the role of my spineless, submissive mother, while I was her blind, spoiled, and abusive son. There were only the two parts. It took several hours to make me up as an Asian, but I didn't have to learn any Chinese dialogue. She had to kneel before me several times, and each time her knees would crack, causing her embarrassment. She was afraid the audience would hear the sound.

I enjoyed working with Miss Wong under Mr. Hinsdale's direction. It was an education in theater. I had no problem with stage fright, because of my experience in radio and before the camera, but I learned a lot about stage presence.

The next year I worked in *City Streets* (Columbia, 1936) with Leo Carrillo and Edith Fellows. Mr. Carrillo, who later played Pancho in *The Cisco Kid*, was a splendid actor. He was descended from an old Spanish family in California. A whiz at dialects, he played an Italian in *City Streets*, a B+ picture. Edith played the sad-faced, handicapped girl with the big, wide eyes. I was her brother, and Carrillo looked after me. I loved Carrillo. He was a warm, sharp actor with a fine sense of humor.

In 1936 I also appeared in *Hideaway* (RKO) with J. Carrol Naish. He was usually cast as a heavy, playing an Italian gangster of the old Chicago bootlegging days. Later he played in *Sahara* with Bogart and appeared in *Down Argentine Way* with Don Ameche. In the fifties he played Charlie Chan on television. Oh, yes: He was Irish, not Italian, but remember, Hollywood is a dream factory. And his roles as a heavy belied the true Naish. He was really a fine, gentle guy.

In addition to Naish, the cast of *Hideaway* included Fred Stone and Marjorie Lord. Richard Rosson directed. The first scene was a trucking shot, walking with Stone, who played my grandfather. In a trucking shot the camera is on tracks and precedes you as you walk. I had two pages of dialogue and had to handle a frog, a creature I detest.

Rosson dressed as an archetypical director, wearing jodhpurs and boots and carrying a riding crop, and that first day he began to shout and browbeat me. I completed my scene, but at the end of the day I was a basket case. I told my mother — remember, a parent had to be on the lot with a minor — and the next day, when Rosson yelled at me, my mother walked on and did her own yelling. If yelling was what he liked, yelling was what he got.

"Stop!" she shouted. "You son of a bitch, don't you ever talk to my son like that again! I'm taking him off your goddamned picture. I have a right to do it, and I won't stand by and see him tormented."

She took my hand and started to walk off. Instant change on his part! He ran after us, saying, "I thought I could get the best out of him."

She turned on him. "No, you can't!" She was scary. I had never seen her like this, nor would I again. "You'll never get anything out of him unless you're polite to him."

We did go back, and what a transformation! He became the nicest guy in the world.

In 1936 I also had a walk-on bit in Universal's *Next Time We Love*, in which Jimmy Stewart and Margaret Sullivan played a couple whose marriage is threatened by their careers — his as a newspaperman and hers as an actress. In my brief scene he sits in a park with a baby, and I walk up and ask, "Is that your baby?" "Yes," Stewart says, to which I reply: "Hmph. Not much of a baby." He looks at smart-mouth me as I walk away.

Then, one day in 1937, my agent got a call from Roach, asking him to send me over. I entered the inner sanctum, but not with the awe I had felt the first time. There he was, in his big chair behind his big desk, and smoking his big cigar. "Hey, Tommy" (that was his voice all right), "how would you like to play the toughie against Alfalfa, Spanky, and the rest?"

I was back!

The dirt floor was still there, as was Mrs. Carter, and the classroom. Everything was much the same. But I had to develop a whole new personality on the screen. I had been "Tommy," a pleasant little fellow. Now I became Butch, the local bully, the kind that Mr. Roach must have had in mind at our first encounter when he asked me whether I liked to fight. Butch is the character for which I am probably best remembered. Which says something about audiences.

In *I'll Take Vanilla*, you may recall, I played the tough guy, and now Mr. Roach brought me back to the *Gang* to cast me in that role in *Glove Taps*. I liked the role and I must have been convincing in it, considering how many fights I had with kids who wanted to prove I wasn't as tough as I seemed on the screen.

One other thing— this time there was no contract and there were no options. Nothing. I was a free agent, on call but completely independent. As such I played Butch in fifteen comedies. I had to develop this new personality, one that would inspire antipathy in the viewers. The script can give you a line or two, people can explain the part, but you have to create the screen character yourself, as every actor knows.

A good director helps. I felt a little resentful at having been let go previously, but that feeling melted instantly under the new director, Gordon Douglas. He was one of the best directors I ever worked with. I didn't work for him, I worked *with* him. He would get down on his knees to be at eye level. Being younger than some of my other directors probably gave him an insight into how kids feel. I could sink my teeth into the part because I had real direction. I wasn't just going to stand around, hands in pockets. I was going to act. Mr. Douglas was loose, but organized. He taught me how to play the role, and when he asked for "more," he got it. As far as I was concerned, Gordon Douglas was the only *Gang* director worthy of the name. He treated me as a star, not an extra. God love him. He was compassionate. He had moxie and drive, and he could get talent out of the kids. He worked on each of us. That's what inaugurated the golden era of the *Gang*.

Douglas directed *Glove Taps*, a one-reeler, released early in 1937. In it I am the new kid in the neighborhood, and with my scruffy pal, the Woim, I take a look at the new school we'll have to attend. As the pupils leave for the day, I tell them I'm the new Big Shot and I'll prove it by licking anyone they want to put up against me. Spanky volunteers Alfalfa, who gets the worst of it in the ring until Porky and Buckwheat, the little kids on the sidelines, knock me out with a loaded glove on a stick.

Glove Taps made it for me. I think Roach and Douglas looked at the rushes and Roach liked what he saw. Maybe it wasn't the rushes, maybe it was the survey cards they passed out at the theater. Or a combination of rushes and cards, I don't know. I do know that I stayed, though Roach didn't have to keep me. No contract meant no obligation to retain me.

It was good to be back with the *Gang*. Spanky's character hadn't changed. The new kid, to me, was Alfalfa. He and I hit it off right away, though you'd never believe it from the parts we played.

Alfalfa barely tolerated Spanky and Darla. Was there a rivalry between Alfalfa's mother and Spanky's over lines for their kids? Spanky seemed to recall that there was. As for Darla, Alfalfa really didn't like her, contrary to rumors that he had a crush on her. He called her "mama's girl," and he told me he didn't like her mother, either. He also didn't like Mickey (Robert Blake) and made no secret of it.

I got along with Sid (the Woim) Kibrick, my sidekick in

many of the films. The younger ones, Buckwheat and Porky, were too little for me to pair with them. They never seemed to take note of the camera, as I recall. They just did what Gordon told them to do. But all of the kids had natural talent, or Roach wouldn't have kept them.

After *Glove Taps* Douglas directed *Rushin' Ballet*, a two-reeler, released in April 1937. The Woim and I break up a marbles game played by Porky and Buckwheat and smear their faces with some handy tomatoes. When Spanky and Alfalfa decide to avenge the little kids, the two bullies chase them into a dancing academy, where they have to join in the program to save themselves. Meanwhile, the Woim and I disguise ourselves and also join the program in progress. We toss Alfalfa into the wings, pretending it is part of our dance, but, as in *Glove Taps*, the little kids, too young to know they should be afraid of us, find a fitting revenge by pelting *us* with tomatoes from their seats in the audience.

The first entirely comic short I worked in with Douglas was *Fishy Tales*, a combination of takes, laughs, and special effects. I mentioned some of the special effects earlier. *Fishy Tales* (released in August 1937) was one of my favorites. When Alfalfa accidentally shoots me with a suction-cup dart I threaten to bounce him around "like a rubber ball." He faints, feigning a dislocated shin bone. Lying in bed, he uses a fish (rubber, of course) in a black sock to substitute as his leg, and invites me to hit it with a hammer to prove that his feeling is gone. However, Gary (Junior) Jasgar sits under the bed, tickles Alfalfa's dangling foot, and releases crabs that attach themselves to Alfalfa. Cats join the fray to add to the fishy high jinks. Leonard Maltin and Richard Bann wrote of my performance that "as the aimless tough Butch, Tommy Bond is delightfully convincing, as usual, and steals all honors again. . . Butch seems to revel in his own scowling villainy, taking sadistic glee impatiently rattling off his lines. . . ."

69

Here was another example of Douglas getting down and working with the kids. His genius was in making us act as if we believed the rubber fish was a real barracuda. "Pound that leg," he told me, and I did. The look of amazement that passes over my face was not ordinary acting — I really got into the scene. I knew, of course, that the fish was a rubber prop, but it truly seemed as though I were hitting Alfalfa's leg, and it surprised me that he wasn't reacting.

In *Framing Youth*, released two weeks after *Fishy Tales*, Douglas used a frog ingeniously for effect. I threaten to beat Spanky unless he keeps Alfalfa out of a radio talent show in which I'm competing. A frightened Spanky tries to persuade Alfalfa to skip the show because of "a frog in the throat" — a real frog, concealed in Alfalfa's scarf. Alfalfa nevertheless sings in the show, the frog provides unintentional croaking accompaniment that charms the audience, and when I try to take revenge on Spanky, he gives *me* a couple of shiners.

Came the Brawn was released in mid-April 1938. Earlier, I told of losing my pants in that one. It really surprised me. I was fighting Alfalfa in a makeshift boxing ring. He doesn't know it's me because I am disguised as "the Masked Marvel." Buckwheat and Porky cut a hole in the canvas, and I fall through. They're supposed to pull off only my Masked Marvel suit, but, unbeknown to the audience, they also pulled off my pants. Meanwhile, Alfalfa is taunting me with "Come up and fight." Alfalfa wins by default.

"Come on up, Tom!" ordered the director.

"You're not getting me out of this canvas. They pulled my pants off!"

Eventually I came out from under the canvas.

The fight was for Darla's affection, but neither of us gets her. She decides to go off with the polite, bookish Waldo because she can't stand us ruffians.

Darla Hood stood out among the girls. She was certainly a

charmer, every little boy's dream of the ideal girlfriend. She was coy, dimpled — just plain cute. When we were youngsters, Darla was often one of the guests at house parties I gave on Zelzah Avenue in Encino. She was a good little trooper, did her work, and was fun to act with. In later years she was a guest on shows such as Jack Benny's comic take-offs of *Our Gang* in which Jack used to take the part of Alfalfa and Don Wilson played Spanky. I believe she also starred with Ken Murray in his Blackout Show at the El Capitan Theater on Vine Street in Hollywood. Still later she took advantage of her three-octave voice to do voice-overs in commercials, in which she might be the Barbie Doll or the Chicken-of-the-Sea mermaid. Unfortunately, I don't know much more about Darla than what is common knowledge — that she had a difficult marriage to a stroke victim who was confined to a wheelchair, making it hard for her to pursue her career. She died of hepatitis at the age of forty-nine.

Shortly before her death she approached the Sons of the Desert, a club that met to perpetuate the memory of Laurel and Hardy, and succeeded in convincing them to include *Our Gang* among their interests, since the *Gang* was also a Roach creation. But she died before the 1980 reunion. I'll have a lot to tell about the Sons of the Desert later on.

Big, redheaded and freckled Leonard Kibrick was the stereotypical bully and played that part before my Butch character was created. (In *For Pete's Sake* he was the nasty kid who broke the little girl's doll.) His brother Sid, after a few early parts as an extra, became the Woim when I became Butch. We worked well together. Sid grew into a tall, handsome man, successful in Palm Springs real estate. We keep in touch, as befits two screen pals.

Gordon "Porky" Lee was a member of the *Gang* in its golden era. He started as a two-year-old and shared "otay" — the mispronunciation of "okay," the only dialogue possible at that age — with Buckwheat. An adopted child, he chose the name Gordon because of his affection for director Gordon Douglas.

In August 1938, I appeared in my last *Gang* short made by that wonderful director. It was *The Little Ranger*, in which Darla stands up Alfalfa and goes to the movies with me. The spurned Alfalfa comes to the movie with Muggsy (Shirley Coates) but he dozes off in the middle of a Western. He dreams I have kidnapped Darla, tied him up, and am threatening to dynamite Darla and him if Darla will not marry me. The craven Darla agrees to be mine. But Muggsy arrives, tosses the dynamite out the window, and saves Alfalfa from my clutches. At which point Alfalfa wakes up, punches me, and goes off with Muggsy.

This was not only the last *Gang* short directed by Gordon Douglas, it was the first made on the MGM lot. Roach had sold us to MGM. Why? Weren't we a successful operation?

We didn't realize it, but financial constraints and a change that was taking place in movie marketing dictated the sale. Roach basically had to get out of producing short subjects.

The major studios, such as MGM, Columbia, Warners, and RKO were setting up their own short-subject divisions in the mid-thirties and block-booking their shorts to exhibitors with the feature-film package. This meant that the market for shorts made by independent studios such as Educational and Roach was drying up. On top of that, a growing number of theaters were screening second features, called "B movies," instead of the usual newsreel, cartoon, and short. So Roach either had to move into feature production or go out of business.

Laurel and Hardy proved successful in features in 1931, but two attempts in 1934 to move other short-subject stars into features didn't fare well. Charley Chase's feature film *Bank Night* did poorly in previews. It was cut down to a two-reeler and released as *Neighborhood House*, after which Roach let Chase go — after seventeen years! *General Spanky*, Roach's feature-length *Gang* film, released in 1936, flopped. The *Gang* was popular enough to be Roach's only surviving short-subject series between 1936 and 1938, the time during which I came back. But the shorts were cut from two reels to one.

Roach never sold Laurel and Hardy, though. Their contracts with Roach expired in 1940 and they decided not to renew, but to produce their own films. Financial support never materialized, so they signed with 20th Century Fox and MGM. Their wartime films were just as inept as the wartime *Gang* films cranked out by MGM.

MGM was big time, the world's largest movie studio, but their lot was much more impersonal than Roach's. It had a regimented, business-like atmosphere. This was definitely NOT "the Lot of Fun." Strangely, the pace was no different, even easygoing — it still took a week to make a one-reeler. But the feel of the place, compared with Roach's, was like the difference between a four-star restaurant and a streetcar diner. MGM, in short, was the Cadillac of the motion picture industry. All the performers, incidentally, were treated with courtesy, regardless of importance, and, being in the *Gang*, I was *somebody* on the MGM lot.

One thing was the same. When Roach sold us to MGM we lost Gordon Douglas as director, but Mrs. Carter transferred to the MGM lot with us. It just wouldn't have been right without her. The *Gang* now got its schooling at MGM, though we had not attended MGM's Little Red Schoolhouse previously. Some actors, such as Mickey Rooney, Judy Garland, and Freddy Bartholomew, grew up at the Little Red. It was rather confusing — probably more for my teachers than for me — to go from public school to studio lot school (and back to public school). The school administration probably hardly noticed, since I was still in the same L.A. school district, but I'll bet the classroom teachers noticed.

As time went on I had other teachers. There was a Mrs. McDonald at MGM. I don't really remember much about her, but I do remember my MGM classmates. There were Mickey Rooney, Judy Garland, and Kathryn Grayson.

I'm often asked about kid stars who weren't members of the *Gang* — Mickey Rooney, for example. Mickey was slightly older and there was a definite resemblance between us, so for these reasons we never co-starred. (Sid Miller, who didn't resemble Mickey any more than an orange does a cherry, starred in every Rooney movie.) There was some competition and some rivalry, between Mickey and me, both personal and professional, but most of it was studio hype. And the rivalry was not unfriendly. While I was making *Let's Talk Turkey*, one of the *Pete Smith Specialties* (two-reel shorts directed by Felix Feist), Rooney was making an Andy Hardy movie down the road. For *Let's Talk Turkey* the prop man had prepared four roast turkeys. Rooney came over to my set and was astonished at the sight. "What are they going to do with all those turkeys, Tom?" he asked.

"I don't know," I answered. "Let's ask the prop man."

The prop man shrugged. "Help yourselves, boys. We're done with them."

So Mickey and I feasted on turkey. We thought it was great.

Besides getting used to the MGM school, I had to get used to a new director. MGM usually appointed executives' sons as directors, giving them shorts to direct as a way to obtain experience. However, a young man who had started out as a messenger boy and had risen through the ranks as sound technician, film editor, and finally to screen tests director, was put in charge of the *Gang*. The young twenty-two-year-old-man was George Sidney. Despite his earlier experience (garnered in only five years with the studio), he was still green when we were given to him. He cut his professional teeth on us and we helped because we were already pros. He knew enough about us to let us act on our own, since we had proven ourselves. George Sidney, a wonderful gentleman, went on to win a couple of Oscars and to become the studio's feature director, producing such wonderful films as *Annie Get Your Gun, Show Boat, The Harvey Girls, Scaramouche,* and *Bye Bye Birdie.* Then Sidney was replaced by Edward Cahn, an OK fellow. But I had been used to working with George Sidney, and it was hard to change when one became accustomed to a director.

In *Party Fever* (released shortly after *The Little Ranger*), Alfalfa, Waldo, and I compete for Darla's company at the Strawberry Festival. We run for junior mayor during Boys' Week and agree that the winner will take Darla to the festival. Campaigning, I throw a giant marshmallow roast for all comers, and Alfalfa goes up in a skywriting balloon. Waldo's uncle (the real mayor) throws the election to him — for an essay on honesty and good government!

Football Romeo, released in mid-November 1938, hinges upon Darla's efforts to persuade a lovelorn Alfalfa to play in a football game against Butch's Assassins. He wins the game and Darla's love.

In *Practical Jokers* (Christmas 1938) the *Gang* plans to sabotage my birthday party by substituting a firecracker for a candle, which was calculated to blow up in my face. My "mom" asks Alfalfa to hold the birthday cake, with the candle on it, while he sings a birthday song. You can guess the result.

The day the party scene was to be shot I found that my dog had been run over and died. I loved that dog. Nevertheless, I had to do a scene in which everyone is happy. The show must go on, so I managed with no visible sadness.

They changed my name several times in this one, incidentally: Butch Rafferty, Butch Burns, then back to Butch Bond.

Taking advantage of the Errol Flynn swashbucklers that were so popular at the box office, MGM released *Duel Personalities* in March 1939. Under the influence of a street hypnotist, Alfalfa thinks he is d'Artagnan. He challenges me to a duel, hoping to see which one Darla rushes to first. But we substitute cap pistols for the real thing — and she goes off with Waldo. As you can see, a great many of the stories boiled down to just one plot: Alfalfa vs. Butch for Darla.

In *Cousin Wilbur* (April 1939) Wilbur — Alfalfa's prissy cousin — persuades the *Gang* to offer insurance for punches and kicks. When I find out about it, the Woim and I ruin the club's treasury by punching everyone in sight. Hollywood illusion reigns once more. Spanky and Wilbur are friends in the film, but in reality we knew that Spanky and Scotty Beckett, who played Wilbur, weren't friends. Perhaps Spanky saw him as a rival.

Two shorts were released in July 1939: *Dog Daze*, in which I run a loan-sharking operation, and *Auto Antics*, in which I sabotage Spanky and Alfalfa's soapbox derby car. Neither of these were developed as well as they could have been. In *Captain Spanky's Showboat* I try to spoil Alfalfa's singing debut because I want the role in Spanky's new production. But when I cut a rope, thinking it will send a chandelier crashing down on Alfalfa's head, it actually loosens a sandbag that knocks me out, allowing Alfalfa to finish uninterrupted.

My last role as Butch was in *Bubbling Troubles*, released in May 1940. Again Alfalfa and I compete for Darla. Alfalfa sees that the dynamite I'm pretending to concoct in my garage laboratory is really a stomach remedy. He drinks it down before the stomach powders have thoroughly fizzed. His stomach swells until he lets out a belch so mighty that his deflation blows down the wall of his house.

During all the time we were making these shorts I was free do other things, being without a contract with Roach. I was given first choice of a *Gang* short and usually took it, but only if it fitted in with whatever else I might be working on. I worked in movies such as *Rosalie* and the *Pete Smith Specialties* that I have mentioned.

Some consider typecasting bad because it presumably limits an actor to a single kind of role. Typecasting never hurt me. Every time they needed a youthful heavy somewhere, they'd say, "What about the guy who played Butch?" If I'd been a pretty boy I probably would have been winnowed out because there were so many of them in the studios. Yet, in spite of being cast as a tough brat, I also played sympathetic parts.

While still with the *Gang* as Butch, I acted in another Roach series, the *Laurel and Hardy* comedies. Laurel and Hardy were the first funny people I worked with. They were kind, enjoyable, and creative. They thought up many of their scenes. Most of their gags have been stolen by other comics over the years.

Blockheads, which came out in August 1938, included

me as a brat — the kid nuisance. The story starts with Hardy reading that a soldier has been found in the trenches twenty years after World War I. No one believes anyone could be so dumb as to remain in the trenches so long. Then Hardy realizes it is his old pal Laurel. He brings his friend home, but Mrs. Hardy walks out, and the boys have to prepare their own dinner, with predictably disastrous results. I am a mean kid with a football and a big, mean father. Laurel and Hardy get tired of my tossing the football about and throw it down the stairs. That's thirteen flights of stairs. My mean Pop makes them go down the stairs and bring it back.

Laurel and Hardy ran the whole gag, as they did with all the gags in this gag-filled film. I was delighted to work with them. I had as much fun as they did. They used lots of special effects — Laurel's finger lighting Hardy's cigar, or an episode I saw put together in which the two adults appeared as little kids in Lord Fauntleroy outfits. They performed in an oversize room with oversize furniture, bathtub, and even door knobs.

I was glad that I had the experience of appearing in a variety of films apart from the *Gang* shorts. Looking back, I have often noted, and viewers have confirmed my notion, that the quality of the MGM *Our Gangs* deteriorated. As long as Butch and the Woim were there, we did our thing, and MGM was happy with it. But the *Gang* kept changing, as it always did. The regulars I had worked with in the Golden Age gradually dropped out. Porky and the Woim played in their last episodes in July and December, respectively, in 1939. Alfalfa played in another seven until the end of 1940. Darla made sporadic appearances in another ten through the end of 1941. Spanky was seen in the next twenty-three until the end of 1942. But Buckwheat starred in all of the next thirty-three, surviving until the series ended in 1944.

After I left, Mickey Gubitosi and Froggy (William

Laughlin) came, and, although it wasn't their fault, it was downhill for the *Gang*. With the outbreak of World War II the films adopted patriotic themes and the kids became miniature adults or tear buckets. Mickey Gubitosi cried a lot. Today he is a fine actor under the name Robert Blake.

I enjoyed all the *Gang* films I was in. My role as a bad guy never embarrassed me. You can't embarrass a bad guy, otherwise he isn't so bad, is he? But by the time I played in *Bubbling Troubles*, I was becoming self-conscious about my size. I had grown, and I knew it. I was taller than most of the others in the cast. The time had come for me to leave at last. I felt no regret, no sadness. I had outgrown the *Gang*. There was no formal termination. I was merely told I wouldn't be called back.

Pete The Pup And Other Friends

Do you remember Pete the Dog? Of course you do. The white dog whose eye was ringed with a circle like a monocle. Pete was a pit bull. He was a gentle, lovable dog who never snapped or growled. You saw us playing with him, mauling him, grabbing his ears, putting our arms in his mouth, and riding him like a horse. And none of it was a camera trick. It was all real. Pete never objected. I would have remembered a dog that snapped or growled, but Pete was a pussycat, so to speak. He never had to be muzzled.

Like the other *Gang* members, Pete had tricks to learn in performing, as when Spanky made his debut in 1932 in the appropriately named *Spanky*. Spanky, only three, was supposed to hit a rubber bug with a hammer. Don Sanstrom, the prop man, had attached the bug to a concealed wire. He pulled the bug away each time Spanky tried to hit it. Bob McGowan kept saying, "Spanky, hit the bug! Hit the bug!" Each time he tried, the bug was yanked away. Frustrated, Spanky yelled back, "If Don will hold the damn thing still, I'll hit it." Striking again, he missed the bug and hit Pete's foot. Pete ran under the bed.

There was a dog role in *Gang* films all the way from Pal the dog in *The Buccaneers* (1924) to Spotty in the very last *Gang* film, *Tale of a Dog* (1944). But the role of Pete with the *Gang*, though over a shorter time period than that, nevertheless made him and the several generations of his successors, the longest-lived character in the series: from *Olympic Games* (1927) until *Pete the Pup* (1938).

The several Petes were very smart dogs. A German trainer named Harry Lucenay had worked with the original Pete, but the later Petes learned their tricks from Tony Campanero, a Neapolitan. He spoke broken English. He handled those dogs by his dominating personality. I remember him looking at Pete and sternly commanding, "Sit!" or "Go!" And Pete would do as he was told. Was it fear, love, or just plain obedience? I don't know.

There were two types of shots with Pete. If he was in a group shot with us, one of the kids would generally walk him with a leash. While we were performing on the set, Tony would be off camera, not issuing orders. But if Pete had a specialty shot, running under a bed or putting his paws over his ears, for instance, it would be filmed by itself, probably when we were in school. Then Tony worked with him. The camera would get a tight shot of Pete doing his specialty, and afterward a group scene would be filmed and the specialty would be inserted.

As a trainer, Tony of course had more animals than Pete in his care. Animal trainer is a job I'd never want. He worked with an organ-grinder monkey named Josephine, who was trained to hold a cup. Josephine had a featured role in Buster

Keaton's *The Cameraman* (1928) and appeared with the *Gang* in *Bargain Day* (1931) and *Mush and Milk*. The studio had to be sure the animals wouldn't turn on us — it didn't want an injury or a lawsuit. It depended on Tony's skill. There was a swaybacked white horse, now that I think about it. I remember a photo of five or six of us on the horse, with his back curving way down. The S.P.C.A. might not approve, but we didn't hurt him. Dinah the mule, known as "Algebra" in *Honky Donkey*, was another animal in Tony's care.

For *Pete's Sake* is my favorite *Gang* movie involving Pete. Leonard (the Woim's brother) deliberately breaks the bedridden Marianne's doll and refuses to do anything about it. Wally and the boys promise to get her a new doll that very day, but we can't come up with the $1.25 it costs at the neighborhood novelty shop. Leonard's seedy dad (actor William Wagner) owns the shop. He offers to trade the doll for Pete. Wally refuses and tries unsuccessfully to raise money by beating rugs. Finally the *Gang* sadly surrenders Pete in exchange for the doll, but accidentally breaks a vase while leaving. Leonard's dad repossesses the doll to cover the cost of the vase. But Pete turns on bratty Leonard and his seedy dad, wrecks the shop and scares them so they beg the *Gang* to remove him. Wally agrees — if they can have the doll. Having no choice, Leonard's dad yields. A last-minute mix-up in dolls is remedied by Pete, who races back, retrieves the right doll from the store, and presents it personally to little Marianne.

The *Gang* wasn't complete without Pete. We were a family. Pete went along with us on personal appearances to charity functions, fundraisers for the Red Cross, rallies for the New Deal's NRA, and a benefit for victims of the 1933 Long Beach quake (Joe E. Brown and Joan Blondell were at that benefit, too). And, there were those personal appearances known as the Orpheum circuit. My mother didn't want me trekking all over the country for one-night stands, so I attended local benevolent appearances, and was never away from home. The studio left it up to us. Spanky, Darla, and Buckwheat hit the circuit, but I bowed out. I don't think I hurt my career. Personal appearances were outside the daily routine. As I said, the routine consisted of memorizing lines, acting, and going to school. When work and study were finished, we played and had lots of fun.

I'm often asked if we were all friends, just as we appeared to be on the screen. Well, yes . . . but some were closer than others. Alfalfa, whose face I was always trying to rearrange and whose nether regions I always threatened to kick on screen, was my best friend.

Carl Switzer was his real name. His family were country bumpkins until they went into vaudeville, singing off-key to a guitar accompaniment. Actually, Carl was born in Illinois. His parents, innocents in Hollywood, somehow finagled a studio interview for him, and Roach liked Carl's face. Alfalfa's only makeup was his Vaseline-twirled cowlick, which he calls his "personality" when a chicken plucks it in *Roamin' Holiday*.

Alfalfa was the youngest of three. His sister Janice resembled him, and so did his brother Harold, though lighter in color. His siblings were nice kids, and Harold sometimes stood in for Alfalfa. Their dad was a handsome man, resembling Tennessee Ernie Ford, and his mother was tall and good-looking.

Alfalfa used to play tricks on the studio. Once he urinated on the floor lights. The hot lights, drying the urine, caused such a stink it was believed a skunk had entered the studio. The adults opened the windows frantically, but never found out about Alfalfa.

He believed he could sing. That's what made him so funny. He thought his off-key was on-key. Of course it didn't help that people on the set told him he had a voice. He took them at their word, though they were joking and knew that the audience would howl with laughter on hearing his rendition of "Let Me Call You Sweetheart" or some other poor, mangled song. I often wonder what he thought when he went to the movies, saw himself on the screen, and heard the audience laughing. Perhaps he believed they were guffawing at his hammed-up facial expression, not his voice. Doubtless he thought it was his rolling eyes that made people laugh. As Darla said more than once, "Poor, poor Alfalfa."

Mrs. Carter tried to make sure we learned. You know the old saw about leading a horse to water. Well, that was Alfalfa. He was Mrs. Carter's bane. He hated lessons and he could think up shrewd schemes — almost anything to get out of school. The rest of us knew we couldn't leave until we had done our classroom assignments and that we could play after we finished them. Alfalfa had to stay in almost daily while the rest of us were free. We felt sorry for him, but Mrs. Carter was adamant that he wasn't going out until his lessons were done. He tried everything, even getting down on his knees, begging, moaning and groaning about his fate (just as he does to Spanky in the clubhouse when I threaten to beat him up in *Fishy Tales*). When she was out of earshot he would mutter: "I hate that woman," or something like that.

It was a good thing we were friends, because even though I had muscles I didn't want to tangle with him. Alf was wiry. He was like coiled steel, and he had a short fuse. He wasn't a bad kid, but he was devilish. He was always in trouble, and if you crossed him, he carried a grudge. This vengeful characteristic remained with him all his life. In 1955, when my wife Polly first met him at a reunion sponsored by *TV Guide*, she liked him, but couldn't understand why he was bad-mouthing Mrs. Carter after twenty years.

Why? She was always fair. It's wrong to hold a grudge that long. Acid, the saying goes, does its greatest damage to the container. Polly, who has great insight into people (after all, she married me), was struck by his outburst. "Boy!" she exclaimed. "He has a terrible temper. He's vengeful. Except about you. He loves you."

"He always did," I replied. "We were natural buddies."

Our families had fun together. We went to house parties. We dressed up on Halloween and went trick-or-treating. Once we went coon hunting in Topanga Canyon. Alfalfa's dad, being a country boy, loved hunting, and the San Fernando valley was still open land, with orange and avocado groves and vacant fields. My dad and I accepted the invitation to go coon hunting. They took their old coon dogs, bloodhound type, in the trunk of their Cadillac and, once out in the country, let them out. My dad was no hunter, but we went along, even though it was dark. Topanga Canyon was still wild in the thirties, with only a few houses here and there. We reached the top of the canyon at midnight and turned the dogs loose. Barking, they chased everything — cats, skunks, other dogs. The few residents turned their lights on, wondering what was happening as the four of us, dressed in old clothes, followed those crazy dogs down into the canyon. At 5 a.m., having caught no prey, we gave up and went home. But dad and I had indeed caught something: poison oak. We never repeated that adventure.

After we left the *Gang*, Alfalfa and I went our separate ways. He played co-pilot for John Wayne in *The High and the Mighty* (1954). We met again at the *TV Guide* reunion in 1955.

At appearances and reunions, when people find out who I am, they often ask how Alfalfa died. There are many stories about what happened, but they are not true. Some have concocted tales of a fight over drugs, and as late as 1992 a friend was told that Buckwheat shot Alfalfa over a drug deal. Not true! In fact, the fight in which he died concerned coon dogs. Apparently he sold a dog or two to a man who refused to pay him when he went to collect the $35 debt. He probably came on with his angry style, and words led to blows. Alfalfa had a knife. The other fellow had a gun and shot him. Alfalfa was D.O.A. at Valley Receiving Hospital in the San Fernando Valley.

The coon dog version can be verified. If you think I'm just covering up for a friend, you can read Alf's obituary as it appeared in the *Los Angeles Examiner* on January 22, 1959.

When people wonder why I didn't know so-and-so from the old days, they forget that there were hundreds of *Gang* kids before I joined the *Gang*. Ernie "Sunshine Sammy" Morrison was one. I didn't meet him until the 1980 reunion. Sunshine Sammy was not only the first African-American Roach star, he was the first member of the *Gang*. Born in 1912, he joined Roach in 1922 for *Our Gang*, the first short. Alert 'til the end, he unfortunately died in 1989.

Many film historians seem to think the color barrier in Hollywood remained high until the 1960s as it did in the rest of the nation. But the *Gang* broke the color barrier long before federal law required it. True, as *Entertainment Tonight* recalled early in 1988, *Gang* shorts showing us going to the same school were cut in some states in the deep South, but we ate, played and attended school together. There was no prejudice in the *Gang*. Some critics may ascribe that observation to rose-tinted glasses, but read what one of the African-American kids recounted to Maltin and Bann: "I think,"

recalled Farina (Allen Hoskins) in 1975, that "even though there was a certain amount of stereotyping of the black kids . . . the kids were shown just as kids, with a cross-section of what makes up American kids, blacks and whites . . . Even the whites were stereotyped. There were the classic fat boy, the freckle-faced boy, the little blonde angel. . . . " This was from the Maltin-Bann book, *Our Gang*, 1977. In their 1992 version, entitled *The Little Rascals*, they quoted Farina as saying he didn't encounter discrimination until he entered the still segregated army in World War II. And Sunshine Sammy Morrison said of Hal Roach that "when it came to black people, the man was color-blind."

In the same vein, a black film historian, Donald Bogle, wrote in 1973 that, while there was stereotyping of black children, "the approach of the relationships of the black children with the whites was almost as if there were no such thing as race at all. Indeed, the charming sense of *Our Gang* was that all the children were buffoons. . . . " And at the 1980 reunion, Buckwheat reaffirmed that "we were all friends, we all got along." Who's going to dispute that?

The bottom line was this: When people are in a series together, animosity isn't tolerated, especially such an irrational animosity as prejudice. In short, we had to get along and it wasn't difficult.

Shortly after the 1980 reunion, word came over the wires that Buckwheat had died. I was saddened by the news, but glad that I'd been able to see that wonderful, sweet guy before he passed on to the great clubhouse in the sky.

Farina was sometimes filmed as a girl, draped in a dress and with his hair in piglet curls. As a result, many fans didn't know his gender when he was little. Buckwheat could probably empathize with that. The same thing happened to him between 1934 and 1935. There were no African-American girl stars in the *Gang*, as I recall, although some extras, such as Stymie's baby sister, did appear from time to time.

Chubby (Norman Chaney) was with the *Gang* before my time. He was Spanky's predecessor. Waldo, the nerd, you may remember, wore a Lord Fauntleroy outfit and pursued Darla. I thought he was nice, but his quiet personality kept us from becoming buddies. Mickey Gubitosi (Robert Blake) came just about the time I was leaving. I remember him as a chronic tear duct. I know now he was a hurting kid. In reality he is a very deep man. Roach needed all types — fat kids, nerds, crybabies. Like us, they were humanity on a small scale.

A good friend today is "Junior" (Gary Jasgar). He played in *Fishy Tales*. You remember, he was the kid with the ugly deadpan face who tickled Alf's foot. He has a spa company in Los Angeles and is doing quite well. I've seen him at reunions, but he confessed to me that he doesn't remember much about the *Gang*, since he was so little when he played in it. But he still enjoys others' memories of him in the *Gang*.

Audience loyalty is one thing that has struck me about the *Gang* and other serials, series, and sequels that I've acted in or seen. MGM sacrificed that loyalty during the forties, when the regulars left and the format deteriorated. The war started, and everyone was into patriotism. The kids were dressed in uniforms or tuxedos but it just didn't work. Mr. Roach had been dead set against any change in the *Gang's* format. The kids were the same type of youngsters he had selected back in the twenties and developed into the thirties, but MGM wanted to use them in a different way. MGM was unable to understand the appeal of natural kids being naturally funny. The MGM shorts became educational films or morality plays, rather than comedies. The result was that movie-going kids could not identify with what they saw on the screen, nor could their parents.

Had MGM been able to devise better stories for the *Gang*, and had it found kids with that natural, unrehearsed spark, the *Gang* could have continued — just as it did when Mickey Daniels, Wheezer, Farina, Jackie Cooper, and others left at about the time I came aboard. Mickey Gubitosi, Janet Burston, and "Froggy" Laughlin just didn't have the natural chemistry of the earlier kids. But MGM also failed to use the plot of protagonist against antagonist for a goal that each sought. Alfalfa (protagonist) vs. Butch (antagonist), vying for Darla (goal) was the whole basis of the *Gang*'s Golden Age. When they made episodes about families and other situations, they failed to hold large audiences. The series needed a good guy and a villain. That's what made it work.

The Big Time

In 1930 MGM started to make a screen version of Sigmund Romberg and George Gershwin's two-year-old Ziegfeld stage show *Rosalie*, and then abruptly stopped. That might not have been good for Marion Davies, who was scheduled to star in this MGM vehicle, but it was good for me. They tried again in 1937, and this time they completed it — with yours truly.

It is surely an understatement that they don't make movies like *Rosalie* anymore and won't ever again. It would take a few gold mines and oil wells to finance an extravaganza like that one. Each year MGM did one or two *major* productions where the budget went out the window and all the big-name actors were in. *Rosalie* was MGM's biggie for 1937. It required the world's largest sound stage. They used a score of cameras, and the sets must have covered acres of the MGM lot. A

Cole Porter score replaced the Romberg-Gershwin numbers. I remember being amazed at thousands of people singing and dancing to Cole Porter's music, or just standing before the cameras.

The producer was William Anthony McGuire, who also wrote the story that went with the spectacle and music. He had learned about extravaganzas from his former employer, Florenz Ziegfeld, the greatest of all producers of stage musicals. W. S. Van Dyke was the excellent, dynamic director for the MGM production. He shouted a lot, but he never browbeat actors.

Nelson Eddy co-starred with Eleanor Powell. The other leads were Ray Bolger (who played the Scarecrow in *The Wizard of Oz*); Reginald Owen (who later played the eccentric admiral in *Mary Poppins*); Ilona Massey (a wonderful operatic singer who was making her debut); Billy Gilbert (who was in the Laurel and Hardy comedy *Blockheads* and *A Little Bit of Heaven* together with me); Edna May Oliver; Frank Morgan (*The Wizard of Oz*); Janet Beecher; George Zucco; William Demarest; Virginia Grey; Jerry Colonna and me. What a stellar line-up! I was still playing Butch in the *Gang* at this time. This was my first big role in a full-length feature movie. It played a great part in my life.

Nelson Eddy acts as Dick Thorpe, a West Point football player. Princess Rosalie (Eleanor Powell) of Romanza, a Ruritania-like country, falls in love with Thorpe when she visits the United States and watches him play on the football field. Thorpe flies to Romanza, only to discover that she is engaged to a prince.

I start out playing Mickey, the football team's mascot, who is supposed to go in if anything goes wrong. But now I become Nappy, the ventriloquist's dummy for Princess Rosalie's father, the eccentric Romanza king (Frank Morgan). I spend most of my time sitting on a couch, but one day I amaze the king by speaking. I convince him that, although I am a dummy, I have been designed as to have the power of speech — and I urge him to approve a marriage between Thorpe and the princess. The king sees that I am really a boy and not a dummy, but he likes what I have said and he agrees to give his blessing to the marriage. He also decides to abdicate in favor of his son. The queen (Edna May Oliver) still thinks I am a dummy, and I surprise her by dancing, which causes her to faint into the arms of the chancellor (Reginald Owen). The movie climaxes with the wedding.

I have some scenes with Nelson Eddy at the beginning of the picture before I return as the dummy. They just don't make actors like Nelson Eddy today — a wonderful man to know and a pleasure to work with. One of the songs was Cole Porter's lovely "In the Still of the Night." Eddy's rendition was haunting. Frank Morgan, the king, was very high strung, but good with us other actors. As for Eleanor Powell, I have the highest admiration for that sweet, warm lady. She was a hard worker and a great dancer. She could keep up with Fred Astaire, as she did in *Born to Dance*, and again in *Broadway Melody of 1940*. They danced together to "Begin the Beguine," and she kept up with all his intricate tap steps. Astaire called her one of the greatest tap dancers ever. Gilbert and Colonna worked so well together that I think they would have made a marvelous team. But to my knowledge this was the only time they appeared together in a movie.

It was while doing *Rosalie* that I learned the intricacies of lip-sync and playback, though I did not have to mime to a playback. Eleanor, Nelson and Ray all had to. The musical numbers were filmed with a live orchestra on the set and had to be shot complete in one take. In those days they used booms to carry the camera and mike. An operator turned the boom and moved it from side to side. On that huge set the camera was high in the air on a crane, lifted to the top of the sound stage. From that distance it was impossible for the mike to pick up all the sounds for both long shots and closeups. Thousands of mikes, taped to everyone and everything, were needed. So playback and lip-sync were essential to get the different sound for long shots and closeups. Therefore the singing, talking, dancing, and tapping were mimed. Because the performers were not exerting their voices, they seemed to dance and sing simultaneously without shortness of breath or problems of pitch, both of which were too evident in the early musicals. For tap dance numbers, such as Eleanor's drum dance, even the taps could be re-recorded on a sound stage and inserted in the final sound track. Lip-sync also allowed retakes to be made of the action and of individual voices that would be merged into the sound track. That's how they achieved perfection.

The Westwood Village Theater, an ornate art-deco movie palace such as was popular in the early thirties, is out near the University of California campus in Los Angeles. There were hundreds of these movie palaces across the country in those days. What's so special about this one? It was and still is used for sneak previews. If you're ever there for a preview you'll be given a questionnaire about your reaction to the movie. There are stubs to tear off by which the answers are computed. The responses help the studio determine whether to make changes before general release.

Nowadays people know what they are going to see at a preview showing. In the past the audience had no advance notice that they would see a preview film, which was simply offered in addition to the regularly advertised feature, in lieu of cartoon, newsreel, and shorts. I was invited to the *Rosalie* preview along with the other performers, and went with my mom. The audience must have wondered what Eleanor Powell, Nelson Eddy and the others were doing there. Anyway, there I was, sitting with my mother in a crowded row when Ray Bolger and Eleanor squeezed in alongside me. Nelson Eddy was on the other side of Eleanor. How can I remember such a detail after more than fifty years? "Tommy," announced Eleanor, "you're going to sit right on our laps." And there I sat, on Eleanor Powell's and Nelson Eddy's laps! It was worth a million dollars to sit on those two laps, surrounded by all those greats. Oh, yes, incidentally, it was a good movie.

When the filming of *Rosalie* was completed, but before the sneak preview, my agent called to say he had a part for me with Wallace Beery in MGM's *Bad Man of Brimstone*. I had always wanted to work with Mr. Beery because I knew that Jackie Cooper had done so, and that any kid who worked with Beery was "made." Great actors and actresses were desirable as working mentors. The great character actors could teach you a lot. They had style.

You may be wondering how I was able to get such juicy parts. Simple. Marcella Rabwin, the head of casting at MGM, was not only a friend, she was married to my doctor, Marcus Rabwin. He was an excellent surgeon at Cedars of Lebanon Hospital, where he was later chief of staff. I became his patient when Eddie Cantor referred me. He was Judy Garland, Al Jolson, and Gary Cooper's doctor. Hollywood, you might say, was one big family.

If you're one of those who take a dim view of nepotism, friendship, and influence, let me set you straight. In Hollywood, people helped cousins, siblings, in-laws and friends, and no one objected. You were expected to take care of your own. I think that complaints about such things in the film industry or anywhere else spring from envy. I wasn't related to anyone in the film industry, but I was accepted.

Another casting director, Jimmy Broderick, put my mother and me on the Union Pacific to go to Zion Canyon, Utah, where the Wallace Beery movie was being shot on location. It took two or three days to reach Zion Canyon by rail. Three hours after we arrived, a telegram summoned us back to Los Angeles. It seemed MGM had to do some retakes on *Rosalie.* My scenes at the end, convincing the king to approve the romance, had been rewritten. I was heartbroken, but *Rosalie* was the biggie that year, so I went back. I never got another chance to play with Wallace Beery. Oh, well, sitting on Nelson's and Eleanor's laps eased some of the misery.

I saw some amazing special effects being created for MGM's 1939 blockbuster, *The Wizard of Oz.* Darla was a little ballerina in the movie. I wanted to be in it also but I couldn't qualify as one of the Lollipop Kids because I was too tall. My friends Judy Garland and Mickey Rooney invited me to watch the filming. What I saw was a sound stage the size of a city block (it is still in use today). It was the site of Munchkinland. It was fantastic, with streams of running water, tiny houses, and huge flowers on the set. In the absence of plastic in those days, the flowers had to be cut from linen, which contributed to make that movie one of MGM's most expensive productions.

When Dorothy's house landed on the Wicked Witch of the East, Margaret Hamilton, playing the Wicked Witch of the West, appeared in a cloud of red, blue, and purple smoke.

I'm not sure which smoke formula was employed, but the filming stopped while she was put in her spot, allowing her to appear magically when the camera rolled again. The arrival of Billie Burke in a bubble as Glinda, the Good Witch of the North, was optically superimposed. Burke, the wife of Florenz Ziegfeld, had earlier appeared in Roach's *Topper*.

The houses in Munchkinland were tiny, but so were the Munchkins. Producer Mervyn LeRoy and director Victor Fleming thought that hundreds of children playing the Munchkins would be impossible to control, so they decided on midgets. Every midget in southern California and as many as they could hire from the rest of North America and Europe were brought to Munchkinland, a.k.a. Hollywood.

They thought children would be impossible to control? Hah! The Munchkins partied in the little houses and just ran amok. The assistant directors went crazy. When you see the Munchkins on the screen, please note that they weren't acting. Chevy Chase's *Under the Rainbow* (Warner Brothers, 1981) was a parody of *Wizard*, based on the midgets' antics.

Why did they behave this way? They were simply bored. Confined in those little houses during long hours of setup and filming, they had to let off steam.

An important special effect, perhaps the oldest one in acting, is makeup. I've had all sorts of experiences with makeup. To make me up as a marionette in *Rosalie*, they used plastic flesh. It was the layering of makeup that gave a ceramic tone to the skin. It took two hours to apply. Plastic flesh feels like the real thing and it has been so refined today that hardly anyone experiences allergic discomfort.

Once I saw one of the greatest makeup jobs ever done. I was acting in Universal's *Little Bit of Heaven*, with Gloria Jean. Boris Karloff was working on the same lot, as Frankenstein's monster in Universal's 1939 *Son of Frankenstein*, with co-stars Basil Rathbone and Bela Lugosi. I wanted to meet Karloff, and one day Gloria asked the obvious. "Boris is putting on his makeup now. Would you like to meet him? Come with me."

When we reached the basement, where the makeup rooms were, all I could see was the monster's back. "I have a friend who'd like to meet you," Gloria announced.

Karloff stood up. From beneath his hideous makeup came a very gentlemanly, British-accented "How do you do?"

He seemed at least ten feet tall. I was five feet two inches. His arms appeared so long. When he held out his hand to shake mine I got a good look at his face, and I was scared to death. I was at least thirteen and fairly sophisticated, but I had never seen *this* kind of special effect. Gloria laughed, because I was trembling — and she was two years younger than I!

The makeup artists worked four hours to apply Karloff's makeup, layering the "plastic flesh" to produce the unearthly ceramic-like flesh tone. Then came his outfit, with those awful heavy boots and the neck electrodes. His pores were clogged, and with all the extra weight he could work only one hour. Then it took another two or three hours to remove it all.

In *Frankenstein* they made up Karloff perhaps only once a week, because acting in all that makeup and gear was so taxing. The set for his "laboratory" had special effects, such as dry ice for steam. The makeup itself was tiring enough, but if he had to fight, throwing people around the lab, it was exhausting. They would shoot, get it over with fast, and turn to other, simpler scenes as soon as possible.

How did I come to be working at Universal? The answer involves a Hollywood practice known as "farming out." I had moved to MGM with the *Gang* and became a free agent. I then went under personal contract to director Mervyn LeRoy in 1937 after the Gus Edwards radio show. LeRoy had started at Warner Brothers. Being under personal contract meant that, although LeRoy had his office on the Warner Brothers lot, I was under contract to him, not WB. Warner, however, could farm me out to other studios. This was a common procedure among all the studios. The big name stars hated it, because when they were farmed out they weren't getting all they could demand for the given role. For example, Warner paid a fixed sum per week under contract. If Warner Brothers lent the individual to MGM for a big movie, MGM paid WB for his or her services, but the actor got only the contracted amount from WB. When MGM lent Clark Gable to Selznick for *Gone With the Wind*, he was unhappy because he could have cut his own deal with Selznick for more money.

While I was under contract to LeRoy I attended school at Warner Brothers for a year. The lovely Lana Turner was one of my classmates. Others were Leo Gorcey, Huntz Hall, Bobby Jordan, Gabe Dell, Billy Halop, and all the kids from the *Dead End* series. Bobby Jordan, who played the "angel" in *Dead End*, didn't act like an angel in real life. He came to school on a motorcycle every day and drove it around the lot. Actually, he was a nice guy. Gorcey was later my neighbor on Fulton Drive in Sherman Oaks. Our teacher was Mrs. Horne. Like Mrs. Carter and Mrs. McDonald at MGM, she saw to it that the child labor laws were strictly observed.

Dead End Kids was originally a Broadway play about kids on New York's Bowery: tough East Side kids who used to dive off the wharves into liquid that was more pollution than water. The kids in that play were taken from the slums and washed up a bit to star on Broadway. The gangster in the play was Humphrey Bogart. Jack Warner saw the Broadway play and decided to make *Dead End* into a movie. He brought the kids to Hollywood, but he hired Edward G. Robinson, and not Bogart, for the gangster role. Bobby Jordan told me that the kids refused to do the movie without Bogart. Warner had to relent, and he brought Humph west for his big Hollywood breakthrough. The kids later made other films for WB, such as *Angels with Dirty Faces.*

I was still under a year's contract with LeRoy, but I wasn't making any movies at WB and my career was stagnating. I kept asking LeRoy when I was going to act for WB. His invariable answer was: "I'm making this one movie first, and you'll be in the next one. I'm going to make four or five this year."

I never did make any movies for Warner. As for LeRoy, he had married Doris Warner, the daughter of Harry Warner. However, he had problems with her uncle Jack and went to MGM in 1938. Louis Mayer lured him to MGM with a fabulous contract, providing an annual salary of $300,000. (To keep MGM's other producers from envious resentment the salary was publicly announced to be $150,000.) LeRoy was a fabulous director. Over the next sixteen years he made more than a score of movies for MGM. Lana Turner, like me, was under personal contract to him when he moved to MGM. He took Lana with him to the MGM studio. Although Lana starred in nearly 30 films, she did only three for LeRoy: *Dramatic School* (1938); *Homecoming* (1948); and *Latin Lovers* (1953).

Despite the stalemate with LeRoy and Warner Brothers, I wasn't idle. I went on to *Five Little Peppers* for Columbia which were typical *I Remember Mama*-genre movies. They were about a family which overcame personal problems through inner strength. There were four of them: *Five Little Peppers* (1939); *Five Little Peppers at Home* (1940); *Out West with the Peppers* (1940); and *Five Little Peppers in Trouble* (1940). The stories were based on Margaret Sidney's book,

The Five Little Peppers and How They Grew. In the first film Polly, the oldest of the sisters, is the adventurous manager of our household while our mother works in a factory. In the next, the family fights bankruptcy and we kids become trapped in a copper mine cave-in. The third gets the kids in trouble in a lumber camp. In the final film we are sent to a boarding school in order to prevent one of the brothers from being taken away by our aunt's court action, and at school we get into all sorts of pranks. You get the idea.

The stars, in addition to me, were my old co-star Edith Fellows, the very talented Dorothy Ann Seese, Ronald Sinclair, Pierre Watkins (with whom I would later play in *Superman*), Charlie Peck, Billy Larson, and Dorothy Peterson as our mother. These were B movies, shot both on location and in the studio in two weeks each. They were black-and-white and ran for about an hour. Charles Barton, a fine fellow, short and comical, directed. He was only about five feet tall, but he had a big heart. Many directors had no acting experience, but he had. He knew how to direct youngsters because, starting as a child actor in San Francisco, he had appeared in several silents as a kid. He left acting about 1924, went into props, and became an assistant director, working under William Wellman on *Wings* (1927). As a favor to Wellman he performed as a comedy-relief actor in the original *Beau Geste* (1939). He was assistant director of many great Paramount films in the thirties, including the Marx Brothers classics *Monkey Business, Horse Feathers*, and *Duck Soup*. He became a Paramount director in 1934. Later he was the top director for such TV sitcoms as *Hazel, McHale's Navy*, and *Family Affair*.

Directors come in all shapes and sizes, and some change with experience. I told you about my encounter with jodhpur-wearing Richard Rosson on the set of *Hideaway*. But Al Rogell, who directed *City Streets*, was the nicest guy and could get anything out of a child actor. There was a cast party at Toluca Lake, and I remember that Edith Fellows, Charlie Peck, and many others were there. Charlie played the rich kid in the *Dead End* movie — the penthouse dweller who is lured down and beaten up by us roughnecks. In the *Pepper* series he played my brother Ben. At the party Al stood up and told us that he loved working with us, but "there is something I have to tell you. I used to be known as an s.o.b. director. I was mean, vicious, rotten. I found it didn't work, so I changed my ways." I swear, you never would have known it.

Back at Warner they were looking for someone to play Jimmy Cagney as a boy in *Yankee Doodle Dandy*, intended as the big movie of 1942. I was sent over because of a physical resemblance to Cagney. I was given a script and told to return for a screen test for the director, Michael Curtiz.

I must remind you that I was sensitive, and if someone didn't like me, it turned me off. I froze and would be unable to perform. I liked most of the directors I worked with. Curtiz, well, I didn't like his methods. He was loud and intimidating. His bad reputation had been sealed in 1929, when he directed *Noah's Ark* and several extras drowned because of his insistence on realism in the flood scenes.

"Mr. Curtiz wants to hear your dialogue," said the dialogue director.

I started out well enough, then stumbled on a word.

"What's the matter? Doesn't the goddam kid know his lines?" yelled Curtiz.

I looked at him, walked away, and told my agent that I never wanted to work with him, even if it meant not being in *Yankee Doodle Dandy*.

Other stars, such as Bogart, Cagney, or Bette Davis, didn't have to tolerate his attitude. He knew they wouldn't take it, so he browbeat the lesser players. You had to swallow it or be blackballed.

That sort of thing still happens today. Directors like Curtiz sense any weakness in a newcomer and pounce on it. They feed on it. Thankfully, most of the directors I worked with were different. Directors like Mervyn LeRoy or Gordon Douglas could bring out the best in a young actor just because they were warm people and calm directors.

Was it just Curtiz's personality? I wonder. Warner always seemed devoid of the human touch. When I was there I had the feeling of not belonging. Although I met great folks there — Bogart, Bette Davis, Kay Francis — it was a cold lot compared to the others. RKO, 20th, Paramount, Columbia, and MGM were nice.

Probably the closest, warmest of all was Columbia, perhaps because it was a small studio. It did have some big names — Rita Hayworth and Frank Capra for starters. There I did all my *Peppers* series, *City Streets*, and the Andy Clyde and Monty Collins-Tom Kennedy comedies. It was a close-knit studio right in the heart of Hollywood, and we all knew each other. It was so small it didn't have a commissary. Most of us ate lunch across Sunset Boulevard at Brittingham's restaurant.

Brittingham's was fabled among radio actors in those days. It was next door to KNX and was the watering hole most actors frequented during the two-and-a-half-hour break between East and West Coast broadcasts. If any of you remember wondering why the West Coast shows sounded a little "loose," well, you can stop wondering now.

I was in a radio show whose cast didn't sound "loose." *A Date With Judy* aired on NBC June 24, 1941, and went on throughout the decade. The story centered around Judy and her girlfriend and their troubles with boys. Ann Gillis played Judy. I was on for the first season as Randolph, Judy's brother.

That was the last time I worked on a regular radio show. About that time the American public became eager to understand what was happening in Washington, especially behind the scenes. Along the same line, I made *Adventures in Washington* (Columbia, 1940) with Herbert Marshall, Virginia Bruce, and Gene Reynolds. It was a story of Senate page boys, and a very good story. It concerned an investigation of a page boy who sells Senatorial secrets. Marshall was a terrific actor. He walked with a limp that was barely noticeable. Reynolds, incidentally, later produced *M*A*S*H*.

In 1942 I played a deaf mute in *Big Town Scandal* for an independent studio, Pine-Thomas. It was the story of a newspaper editor (Philip Reed) and his assistant (Hillary Brooks) who organize a street gang into a basketball team. My part was one of the most difficult I ever played, since I couldn't talk and had to communicate solely by pantomime. I was used to being active in a film; to pantomime was a very different experience. I had to learn sign language, with the help of a tutor.

World War II began in 1939, but the world-shaking events of those twenty-seven months before Pearl Harbor really bypassed my life. When the Japanese attacked Pearl Harbor and we were finally in the war, I was fifteen and having problems of my own.

My parents separated.

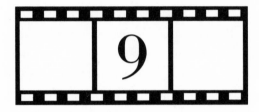

War Duty

I don't think the Hollywood life was responsible for my parents' separation, nor do I believe that they grew apart. We sold our nice home in Encino, and Dad moved to a club in Los Angeles. Mom took Sis and me to an apartment in the Afton Arms on Franklin Avenue in Hollywood. Grandma never really liked Dad and had done her share to encourage the split. Those were the saddest days of my life.

During this tragic time, a very kind man, the Afton Arms manager, took a fatherly interest in me. He used to take me to Griffith Park to visit the observatory, hike the park's many trails, and let me practice my tap dancing in the basement of the apartment house. I was taking tap lessons from Louis DePron, Donald O'Connor's teacher, and I could tap away my depression, at least temporarily.

Thank God I was still at the Columbia studio even though I was not working. Mrs. Barclay was my teacher there when this family tragedy occurred. She was a wonderful lady who loved me and was always there to help, both psychologically and professionally. She was a kind, caring individual who took a genuine personal interest in her students.

She had much influence on the movie lot. If she heard that a picture was under consideration, she would call my mother and suggest: "Tommy should try out for it."

Academically, she helped enormously by assisting in the transition to public school. Even though we were enrolled in the Columbia Studio private school, we went to public school or another private school when we were out of a contract, and she helped to make the connection.

I first tried a private school after Columbia, but it was much like the studio school, with more of the same type of kids — the kind who could only talk show business, and who had no life beyond Hollywood. I realized that Hollywood wasn't everything and I wanted to experience reality, not Tinsel Town make-believe. I decided to go to public school, to be an ordinary person and get my life together.

I had to adjust to regular school again where kids brought bag lunches, went through a full day (much longer than the minimal three hours) and had lots of activities I had never been exposed to. I was apprehensive about the welcome I'd get, remembering how the kids at Encino wanted to fight me because I played Butch. But it was okay. My father told me: "This is the real world, Tommy; I'll help you cope, but you've got to do it yourself." That doesn't sound too encouraging to a boy, but it's necessary if the boy is to become a man.

My parents were separated about eighteen months, and during that time my sister and I worked hard to reunite them. After the separation, Mom began to miss him. God knows I missed him. Christmas? Birthdays? They just weren't the same.

Jane and I visited him once a week. We'd go out somewhere with him, and then I'd hit him with: "Dad, do you still love her?"

"Yes," he'd respond, "but it's up to her."

Then I'd work on her, until finally she said, "You know, we never should have separated." Did she have to convince me?

During those months I never forced the issue. I just tried to make her realize how lonely she was without him. Well, damned if I can't cure a rainy day! They reunited! We moved to a house on Fulton Avenue in Sherman Oaks, and they lived happily ever after for the rest of their lives.

I had been attending LeConte Junior High in Hollywood. Jane and I had become somewhat closer by that time. She was at Canoga Park High School, working on the school paper and being very big in school politics. Naturally, she wanted me to go there from LeConte. I tried Canoga for one semester, but didn't like it. It was too rural for me. I wanted a city school, like Van Nuys High. A drawing card for Van Nuys was that it offered R.O.T.C. Each day brought me closer to the draft. Anyone with R.O.T.C. training would have an edge when he had to go into the service. I entered Van Nuys in 1943, became a cadet captain, and enjoyed two years there.

Hollywood, meanwhile, had enlisted in the war effort. When I was seventeen, Republic made *Man from Frisco* as a contribution to that effort. It was a ninety-minute film with Gene Lockhart. The movie was filmed at the Chatsworth railroad station, the San Pedro harbor and shipyard, and Republic's back lot. Though I expected to be drafted, I went to take my screen test at Republic. The actors all had experience that fitted them for their parts.

The plot was simple: Mike O'Shea plays Matt Braddock, a thinly disguised Henry Kaiser, the famous shipbuilder of that era. He comes to town to straighten out and modernize a shipyard that is building prefabricated vessels for wartime service. The town organizes against him and his innovative methods. I play Russ Kennedy, "the Professor," Braddock's only ally and a heavy in my family. Ann Shirley plays my sister, and Dan Duryea, her boyfriend. My dad (Gene Lockhart) and I argue about the modernization plans. Pearl Harbor puts an end to the arguing within the family and with the townspeople. I give Braddock the idea of lifting the entire superstructure onto the ship's deck, but because of a welding flaw all 180 tons of it drop on me. What a death scene! The welding job is corrected, the ship is named after me and finally launched. Braddock goes on to build other shipyards, and America wins the war with the help of Liberty and Victory ships. I probably had my best lines in that movie, but they were so short!

Lockhart and I hit it off, just like that! "Come into my dressing room," he invited, "and let's go over the dialogue." He gave me tips and clues for the part.

Robert Florey, a Frenchman who wrote books about Hollywood, was director. He was taking a chance giving me a role atypical of what I'd played before. As a director, he gave help and guidance. If you made a mistake, he let you go on, but then took you aside quietly and suggested "I'd like to see you do. . . . " After we tried the scene in one or two takes, he and Lockhart agreed that I was the one for the part. I looked and acted the part. I was walking on air — everything was falling into place. Only a minor detail stood in the way — Harry Cohen, the producer, hadn't confirmed it yet.

I heard nothing for three weeks. Then I called my agent and heard the bad news that Cohen had picked a fellow he'd seen on Broadway.

My career was taking a nosedive. I had had everything in Hollywood, and now suddenly I wasn't wanted.

But even the blackest cloud has a silver lining. Two weeks later, the phone rang just after I got home from classes at Van Nuys High. Republic's casting director was on the line.

"Tom, come right over — you got the part!"

Confusion on my side. "I thought someone else got it."

Panic on his side. "No questions! Just get here. We're waiting on the set."

I hopped in my car and drove over. My mother agreed to meet me there.

I walked onto the set of a dining room scene. Lockhart, Dan Duryea, Ann Shirley, Braddock, and Ann Shoemaker (who played the mother) were all sitting around the table, tapping their forks in boredom. Again I asked what had happened, but was told to get together with the dialogue director immediately. Well, I went over the dialogue, sat down, and we got it in a couple of takes.

"Thank God, it's a wrap!" shouted Lockhart. "We've been sitting around this set for three days."

Still confused about my apparent good fortune, I asked Lockhart why I had been chosen and not the other fellow.

"I told them!" he boomed. "I told them you were the one. Cohen finally got wise and called you up." The next day Cohen apologized.

My performance as Russ Kennedy in *Man from Frisco* was my greatest role up to that time, and certainly my best part in a straight role.

I've spoken of the Sons of the Desert, a group whose goal is to perpetuate the memory of Laurel and Hardy and *Our Gang*. In 1992, I attended a Sons of the Desert meeting in Las Vegas. One of the guests was Vera Ralston, who had been married to the owner of Republic. I had never met her, but at this gathering the lovely lady looked at me and announced for all to hear, "You were one of the stars in *Man from Frisco*. Oh, you were wonderful!" Then she turned to the entire group and declared, "I loved that man!"

After *Man from Frisco* was released, I was certain that things would get better, but there was another ebb in my career.

In 1944, I had a part in a cute scene in MGM's *Twice Blessed*, a B+ movie starring Preston Foster and a couple of blonde girls known as "The Wilde Twins." In the movie, they were certainly typecast: identical twins who sell kisses at a charity bazaar. The twins are competing, and when I wander in, one of the girls tries to entice me. I tell her that I've promised my business to the girl in the next booth. Ever confident, she says, "Try me," and plants one on me, back-bend and all. When she's done, I say, "To heck with Josie," and back to it we go. A cute little movie.

The cute and innocent things in life were coming to an end. I turned eighteen in my last semester in high school, in the autumn of 1944. I was quite aware that either I would enlist or be drafted. Only my high school student status had kept me out of uniform. All over America, guys who turned eighteen would graduate one night and be in the service the next.

During my last semester, the war was going well for the Allies. The U.S. fleet crushed the Japanese fleet at Leyte, and Americans invaded the Philippines. North Africa was completely liberated. The Russians had pushed the Germans out of Russia and into Poland. The Americans and British had liberated Paris and were heading for Germany. And then, on December 16, 1944, the Germans counterattacked in the Battle of the Bulge. For eleven days they tried to halt the Allied western advance. They failed, and the Americans crossed the Rhine. Five months later, the war would be over in Europe, and three months after that, the Japanese would surrender.

It sounds exciting now, but it wasn't. It took men to do all of this. Men got killed and had to be replaced. That's what was in store for us when we graduated. If you were a warm body, they took you. I had passed my pre-induction physical twice (how wonderful!). Why twice? I took my first physical when I turned eighteen, as required, but got a student defer-ment. I graduated a half year later, and since it was slightly more than six months since my first physical, I had to take another. You know the routine . . . look at the moving finger, let's see your tonsils, cough. I was certifiably warm. It looked as if it might be the Army for me.

About the time of the Battle of the Bulge, I heard a radio spot that said one could still join the Navy even if he'd passed his Army pre-induction physical. After his terrible experi-ences in the First World War, my dad was concerned for me and encouraged me to avoid the Army at nearly any cost. Here was an alternative way to serve.

I called the Navy recruiting office and a clerk told me to come to Los Angeles and be prepared to spend the morning taking tests. I went with a buddy. We were promised that if we passed the aptitude tests we could become Navy air crew-men. It sounded great, but we were only high school gradu-ates.

My buddy failed after the first test and was excused, along with several other men. I had never seen some of the exam stuff. There were college grads there. Test after test winnowed the group to me and five others. We were told to come back for our physicals in the afternoon (the two I'd already taken

110

for the Army — same government, same war — didn't count). I'd passed! I called home, and Dad was relieved.

Soon after, I received my "greetings" from Uncle Sam and reported to Fort MacArthur. There I stripped down and stood before a panel of Army, Navy, and Marine officers. The Navy and Marines had first choice; the others went to the Army. When the Naval officer asked me what made me think the Navy would want me, I announced, "Sir, here's my letter of directed assignment." The card with my name was thereupon stamped *NAVY*, and I was told to wait in the barracks until I was given an assignment. I waited. Most of the fellows in the barracks were called out to receive Army uniforms. A sergeant came in. I asked him what to do. "Huh? Go home. You're Navy." When I got home, Dad said, "Great, just wait for your call."

A week later MGM phoned. Marcella Rabwin, the casting director, was on the phone. "Tom, you did a great job in *Twice Blessed*. We want you in another film."

I told her I was in the Navy and waiting for orders that might arrive at any time.

"Don't worry," she assured me. "That could take weeks. Come on down and work until you have to go."

I got the part. Shooting was to start the next week.

I went home and started mowing the lawn, but Mom called out, "Tommy, there's a call for you."

I picked up the receiver to hear, "Is this Thomas R. Bond, Serial Number 8819920?"

"Yes."

"This is the Navy." Really? Who else would address me by my serial number? "Report to Union Station to leave for the Memphis boot camp next Thursday morning."

Au revoir to MGM! Union Station, here I come, and hello, Memphis.

In Memphis, we were given tests for assignment: radio

man, aviation machinist mate or ordnance (gunner). All would fly in the big planes — PBYs, PBMs, or the terrible TBMs, torpedo bombers. The PBYs and PBMs were two-and four-engine, respectively, submarine reconnaissance planes with a five-man crew. I passed all three tests and chose mechanics' school. I'd always been interested in mechanical things, working on my own cars and such. I was sent to Norman, Oklahoma, for twenty-five weeks of mechanics' school. You know what they say about the military — travel and see the world.

At Van Nuys High School, I had graduated as an R.O.T.C. captain and battalion adjutant. At Norman they called for anyone with R.O.T.C. training to step forward. I knew that one should never volunteer for anything in the military, but I stepped forward anyway. They apparently liked the way I gave commands, so they made me company commander. I got to march the men of Company 40 to school and chow, and didn't have to stand watches.

Since childhood I'd had sweet-induced cavities, so at Norman I went to the dentist. He looked at my card and then at me and asked, "What did you say your name was?"

"Thomas Bond."

"You weren't in *Our Gang*, were you?"

"Yeah."

"You know who I am, don't you?" he asked.

"No, sir, I don't."

"I'm Fern Carter's son."

"Mrs. Carter's son?"

"Yes. I'm the base dentist. Let's get you fixed up."

He was as good as his word and did a terrific job fixing all my teeth. All the while we — he, actually — talked about his mother and the *Gang* days. I felt better about being in the service. Here was a link to my past.

After about ten weeks at Norman, I caught a bad cold. The dispensary doctor lanced my left ear for fluid. I was given some pills for the pain and sent back to my routine. But the pain became worse, with swelling and a fever. The doctor didn't prescribe antibiotics. It worsened, and then one night I passed out and woke up in the base hospital with a 104 degrees fever. The hospital doctor, one Dr. Edgerly, a Cagney-faced redhead, told me the infection was due to a dirty instrument.

It was pretty much touch-and-go for a week, with pools of pus coming from the ear and a horse shot in the butt every three hours. The Navy summoned my mother from California. Would I live or die? They really didn't know, but after three days there was some recovery. I was hospitalized for ten weeks. Dr. Edgerly saved my life, but I still have trouble with that ear, although it never really affected my career in later years.

While I was laid up, I missed the training that I would have received in Company 40. I was reassigned to Company 50. Meanwhile, my old Company 40 went on to a flight squadron in Pensacola, Florida. On December 5, 1945, six planes — five TBM-3 Avengers and one Martin Mariner Flyer Boat — with a total crew of twenty-seven, flew out from Fort Lauderdale. Three-and-a-half hours later the mission flight leader radioed back:

"We seem to be lost . . . Have enough fuel for 75 more minutes . . . Can't tell whether over the Atlantic or Gulf . . . Not sure, but think we are 75 miles northeast of the Banana River Naval Air Station."

These were the last words heard from the squadron. For five days, dozens of ships and planes combed an area of 380,000 square miles and didn't turn up anything. Not even an oil slick. "The Bermuda Triangle" had swallowed them up.

Years later, when my son and I went to see *Close Encounters of the Third Kind* (Columbia, 1977), he piped up at the sight of the Naval air squadron, "Dad, that was your squadron!" It would have been.

Because of that experience — the ear infection, hospitalization and transfer — I believe in predestination. God has plans for everyone. Obviously, He didn't want me to disappear in the Bermuda Triangle. I only hope that I have spent the past fifty years fulfilling His plans for my life.

I never went into battle, except for my life in Norman. The war ended, but I had to stay in the Navy. I was told that if I wanted to enter the air corps I'd have to sign up for an additional two years. No, thank you; Hollywood and big bucks were beckoning. To fill the time that I still owed, they sent me to Chicago for Storekeepers School, and then to Terminal Island, California. They had me drive an ambulance in Long Beach, then sent me to the National City repair base where I disposed of surplus war material. I was able to spend weekends at home.

In July 1946, I was free. Not only free, but free to go to college. . . .

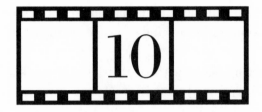

College Days

A fter the war, the United States government decided to show its gratitude to those who had served in the armed forces. It enacted the G.I. Bill of Rights. Among other things, the G.I. Bill enabled millions to go to college. Me, too.

I enrolled in Los Angeles City College as a theater arts major in 1946, and two years later, as I shall relate, I entered the television department being set up at the then newly organized L.A. State College.

L.A. City had a high reputation in theater. It graduated many star character actors like Donna Reed, Alexis Smith, and Hugh O'Brien. Though I played with Anna May Wong in *The Sweetmeat Game*, I had never had formal classroom stage training. I realized that to be a well-rounded actor, I would need it as well as my radio and motion picture experience.

I had excellent teachers at L.A. City. There was Dr.

Eastwood, the helpful dean of men, Dr. Carmichael, Jerry Blunt, and Dr. Guardemal. Dr. Harold Turner, the head of the theatre arts department, was marvelous. He knew theater, and he was a tough driver. It was the best training I ever had. We started at the bottom, making sets and scenery. From there we went on to working props, stage managing, and acting.

The acting began with small parts and worked up to big ones. Dr. Turner had us do a weekly six-minute scene, produced and propped on our own. We went on stage and put on the scene for him and our classmates, and were graded on the spot. Forget your lines and you'd hear, "Curtain, please." That was the equivalent of getting into an accident when you are taking your driver's license test.

I think the best part I had in any of the plays we did was George, the young husband in Thornton Wilder's *Our Town*. To play any of the characters in *Our Town* required real talent. I had a sense of pride about this achievement.

I had other classes, apart from theater studies. One of the interesting teachers was my psychology professor, Donald Powell Wilson, the author of *My Six Convicts*. He told us about interesting cases he had dealt with, such as a girl who shined non-existent armor. A Joan of Arc complex, he called it. One could always count on him for fascinating stories. I loved the class, but I was lucky to get a C. Why? Well, the tests weren't on the fascinating, strange cases. They were on the textbook — Freud, Jung, *et al.*

During my college years I had to work on a movie occasionally. The teachers were most cooperative. Even though I had to take two or three weeks off for a movie job, they gave me full credit. There was one exception, a geography instructor who took personal offense if you did anything to advance your career outside of class.

"As long as I keep up with my studies, take the exams,

and get good grades, what's the difference?" I asked.

"You'll be missing the lectures," he replied.

Frustrated, I demanded: "Give me the textbook and the test, and we'll see."

I was carrying a B+ in the class. He let me take the test — and graded me F on the final exam. My test was on footnotes in the book! Example: "How far does a llama travel in a day?" The correct answer was eight to ten miles. I puzzled over that one, then wrote: "It depends on the female." The teacher took umbrage at that, but I went to the dean, who pressured him to give me a C for my final grade.

Despite this geography pedant, I made out all right. The G.I. Bill required that you maintain a B average. I came out with a B+/A average. More importantly, I learned a lot about theater, staging, and acting before an audience without a script in hand. I'm still learning. When you stop learning, you start dying.

I worked in several movies while I was in college. In addition to starring in the original *Superman* series, I acted in *Any Number Can Play*, *Tokyo Joe*, *Battleground*, and two films in the *Gas House Kids* series.

Gas House Kids (Producers Releasing Corporation, 1947) brought me together with Alfalfa once more. Producers Releasing Corporation decided to do the series, and we made two films, back-to-back: *Gas House Kids Go West* and *Gas House Kids in Hollywood*. The *Gas House Kids* echoed the *Our Gang* days, but Alfalfa and I were the only *Gang* members in the films. They were B-type pictures, not great, but a lot of fun to do. For this series, I was still the tough Butch, but I was now Alf's sidekick.

Any Number Can Play brought Mervyn LeRoy back into my life. MGM brought out this movie in 1949, with Clark Gable as the star. LeRoy directed. I had been under contract to him at Warner Brothers, you remember, but I didn't see him for years after he went to MGM and dropped me in favor of taking Lana Turner there. Then I went to a cattle call for a part in *Any Number*. At a cattle call about 150 hopefuls, all the same age, all seeking the same part, appear on a sound stage. The producer and director pick the ones they want. The others go home, and the lucky candidates read for the part.

I didn't know Mervyn would be the director. He walked down the line, stopped in front of me, and said, "Hi, Tommy."

"Hi, Mr. LeRoy. How are you?"

He dismissed the others, took me to his dressing room, laid out the story, and asked, "Do you want to play the bully or his friend?"

"I want the mean guy."

Mervyn was one of the smoothest and most talented directors I ever worked with. Gable played Mr. King, a casino owner, protective of his son (Daryl Hickman). Alexis Smith was Mrs. King. I played Mike, a college sport. Young King dislikes his father's casino business and resents the father's support and protectiveness as interference. A climactic moment occurs in a restaurant (where Art Baker plays the manager) on prom night. Young King comes there with his date. A crowd of college sports stars and girls are celebrating. I am among them. I saunter over to King's table and ask him to take us to the casino. He refuses. I start a fight with him and it becomes a free-for-all. The police raid the restaurant. I find myself sitting in jail, smoking with the others as we await release to our parents. King becomes reconciled with his father, who bails him out and takes him home.

I had small parts in two films about the war. In Columbia's *Tokyo Joe* I played a staff sergeant in the provost marshal's office at Haneda Air Force Base in occupied Japan. There I take Humphrey Bogart's fingerprints. In *Battleground* (MGM, 1949), a story about the Battle of the Bulge, I played an Army courier.

William Wellman, the director, was a stickler for realism, though not as extreme as some other directors. The battle was fought in the Black Forest in December, remember. Outside, in the real world of Los Angeles, it was 101 degrees in the shade, while on the sound stage, the same one used for *Wizard of Oz*, Wellman ordered the temperature reduced to 30 degrees. Not only was our breath frosty, the stage was buried in four to six feet of gypsum snow, and contained full-size pine trees, overturned tanks, half tracks, guns, and dummies for dead bodies. A huge fog machine, called a Mole Richardson Fog Maker, created a wintry mist. Rather than the standard dry ice (such as you'd see in the first scene of *Hamlet*), they burned mineral oil through hot plates and forced it through the ventilation ducts without irritating our lungs.

James Whitmore, Ricardo Montalban, Van Johnson, and Doug Fowley were among the actors in the film. Wellman's every other word was unprintable, and therefore he wouldn't allow women on the set. He made the actors live on stage for several days to get that grizzled warrior look.

In my scene I was to run up with a message about Germans coming down the road. Wellman wanted me to look sweaty, even in that frosty weather. It would have been simple to spray me with a spray bottle, but he wanted real sweat. How to do that in 30 degrees?

"Put on your pack and run around the stage several times."

"Wait a minute," I retorted. "I got out of the service!"

Still, I was being paid, so I ran around three or four times, huffing and puffing and working up a good sweat I could hardly remember my lines, but he was satisfied.

"Great! Let's roll!"

At least there weren't explosives going off under my feet.

One of the funniest incidents in my acting career took place while I was in college and working in *Hot Rod*, a 1950 Monogram movie directed by Lewis Collins. It was a B picture, a fifteen-day wonder. It was about those souped-up Model A's with a V-8 engine, used for racing. My friends Jimmy Lydon, Gil Stratton, Jr., and Myron Healey played in it. Stratton was also a sports commentator, Lydon was the original Henry Aldrich in the movies, and Healey was a fine leading man, character actor, and writer. Also in the movie were several gals and Myron Welton.

Welton and Healey, though sharing the same first name, were as different as night and day — and so were others' perceptions of them. Welton got on everyone's nerves because he talked constantly, bragging about how many women were in love with him. We had to tolerate him while the movie was being filmed, but near the end Jimmy Lydon hatched a plan.

Jimmy gathered Gil, Myron Healey, and me. "This guy is driving us crazy," he said. "We're going to fix his wagon. An attitude adjustment, you know?"

There were no dissenters.

We set him up.

On the last day we shot a courtroom scene with a jury of extras. The actors, the director, and the crew were in on the setup. Everyone except the extras and Welton.

As we were shooting the last scene, the phone rang and a page off-stage called for Myron Welton.

"Yes, I'm Myron Welton."

"Oh, Myron," moaned a woman's sexy voice, "I've admired

you for years. I'm in love with you. I've seen every movie you've made. I want to meet you. Please, oh, please come up to my apartment tonight."

The speaker gave her address, and Welton spent the rest of the morning swaggering and bragging.

Healey had many friends among the stunt men. The caller was a stunt's girlfriend.

When we finished the scene, everyone but the extras and Welton knew we had completed the movie. The director called out, however: "OK, we're going to do one more shot." Nothing was happening, of course, but it looked as if the scene was being filmed.

Healey played a policeman in that scene. Welton was in the witness chair. All at once the door to the set burst open. Two studio guards were holding onto a big bruiser who was roaring like an enraged bull elephant.

"Let me go!" yelled the bruiser. "I'll kill him! I'm gonna murder him!"

"What's the trouble?" stage cop Healey asked.

"I'm looking for a guy named Myron!" announced the bruiser.

"My name's Myron," admitted Healey.

"Oh, yeah?" And with that the bruiser decked him with one of the loudest stage pows I'd ever heard.

Healey sat on the floor, rubbing his jaw, and acting confused and angry.

"Wait a minute. I don't even know you! Why did you hit me?"

"Isn't your name Myron Welton?" inquired the bruiser.

"No," Healey truthfully answered. He turned and pointed to the witness chair. "*That's* Myron Welton."

Welton looked as if he were going to die in that chair. He shriveled up as the bruiser lunged. Two guards grabbed the bruiser, who was actually a stunt man, and pulled him toward the door. The extras were screaming wildly at the scene they had just witnessed.

As the bruiser left he warned Welton, with raised fist, "I know you tried to steal my girl! You may get way with it for now, but you better not show your face outside these studio walls tonight!"

Chaos among the extras, fear and trembling in Myron Welton, and a silent acknowledgment of a great acting job from the rest of us.

Jimmy stepped up as Myron Welton's dearest friend. "Golly, Myron, we'll protect you. We can't let this happen."

"You've got to protect me! Call the police!" wailed a panicky Welton.

Jimmy tried to reassure him, "We'll take care of it. We've called the police."

Some other stunt men, buddies of Myron Healey, pulled up, dressed as police, in a fake black-and-white used for the movies.

Jimmy, sounding relieved, reassured Welton, "Myron, you're OK. We've got a police car pulling up and we'll make sure you get out unseen. In fact, we're not even going to put you in the car. You're going in the trunk."

"Anything!" Welton shouted.

So they put him in the trunk and drove for three hours out to the Mojave Desert, where they let him out.

He apparently got back to Hollywood, because later in 1950 he was in two other Monogram quickies, *Military Academy with That Tenth Avenue Gang* and *The Vicious Years*. I haven't heard of him since, and to this day Myron Welton never knew that this had all been a gag. I wonder if he learned his lesson?

For years after that, whenever I'd meet with Jim or Gil or Myron Healey, we'd burst out laughing with the memory.

The movie? Oh, yes, *Variety* named me as one of those

who "acquitted themselves satisfactorily."

Anyhow, you'd need Superman to keep an eye on guys like that. Now, about *Superman* . . .

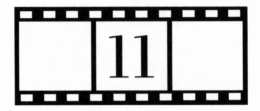

Superman

In 1934, Jerome Siegel and Joe Shuster, two young Cleveland men, combined their talents to create a new comic strip, "Superman." Four years later, Action Comics bought it and that, unpredictably, started an institution. More than five decades later we can look back at hundreds of Superman comic books, thirteen years of radio shows, three novels, seventeen animated cartoons, a Broadway musical, a TV series of more than one-hundred episodes, an animated cartoon series of sixty-nine parts, five feature films and two movie serials of fifteen installments each.

During my freshman year at L.A. City in 1946, I was called by the Mitchell Hamilberg Agency which represented me. Hamilberg handled some big names: Gene Autry, Deanna Durbin, Edgar Bergen and Charlie McCarthy, Gloria Jean, W.C. Fields, and William Tracy, among others. Tom Rooney at the Hamilberg Agency told me that Sam Katzman was planning to create a *Superman* serial at Columbia. "It's a good part," he assured me. "Third lead. You really ought to go out for it."

"Get me the interview and I'll do the rest," I replied.

Lord, I thought, what an opportunity! Only a month out of the Navy, and one of the lead roles in a big show!

Sam Katzman, the producer, and his brother Dave, the associate producer, interviewed me. (If you're not familiar with the Katzmans, Dave's son, Leonard, became the producer of *Dallas*. In 1946, however, Leonard was second assistant director, an important sounding title for the man who does the menial tasks, such as working with stunts and handling payroll.)

Sam got right to the point. "You have a great face, Tom. You have the experience. We really want you for the part — if you want it."

"Sure." What else could I say?

"Well," he started, "we can't pay what you're used to. We're on a low budget. But I can guarantee four weeks of work and third lead."

"That'll be fine," I assured him. I had to get back to work. I had established a salary level of $500 per week for myself, so I would be taking a 50% cut, but I needed a job, the exposure would be great, and the part was a very respectable one.

Sam was happy. "We'll get in touch. Send in your agent."

Tom Rooney went in to negotiate for me, and I signed the contract for the role of Jimmy Olsen in the movie serial *Superman vs. the Spider Lady*. There was a nasty sequel, however, to Rooney's representing me.

During the filming of the *Superman* serial, the Katzmans were always out at the location. Sam was a great guy, a real prince, loyal to those who worked for him. He had lots of experience directing serials. He was also a funny guy. He wore a porkpie hat, sat in the director's chair, and used a cane to goose anyone who walked by. Then he'd laugh raucously. A strange sense of humor — but he was funny, gagging with you, making jokes, always laughing. He and his wife loved to play the horses.

Dave, on the other hand, was a serious fellow, and he turned out to be a good friend. On the second day, Dave called me aside. "You're doing a good job, Tom," he started, then paused. But I have to tell you something. How do you like your agent — not Mitch, but his legman, Tom Rooney?"

"He's OK, I guess."

"Well, when we wanted you and he came in to negotiate the contract, he tried to sell us William Tracy."

I was astounded. "You're kidding!"

"No," he replied. "I'm afraid not. As friend to friend, I think you should know. We didn't want Tracy, we wanted you."

Tracy was about my age. He had played character parts in films like Jack Benny's *George Washington Slept Here*, *See Here*, *Private Hargrove*, and quite a few others. I had often seen him at auditions for the same role, as he was also handled by Hamilberg, but it is absolutely forbidden in the ethics rules of Hollywood to put two of your clients on the same interview. Sam Katzman had invited me there; Rooney was supposed to be a legman, not an agent, for Hamilberg. In other words, he handled the actor Hamilberg told him to handle. I was booked for the interview, Tracy was not. Perhaps Tracy would get more per week than I would and Rooney jumped at the chance of a percentage of bigger bucks. In any case, this was an unethical breach of a fiduciary relationship. Translated, it could get him *and* Hamilberg into very hot legal waters.

The shock of this betrayal bothered me the rest of the day and into the night. I called Mitch and reported my con-

versation with Dave Katzman. I then gave Mitch an ultima-
tum — either Rooney goes or I go. Hamilberg was a big agency,
with a reputation to uphold, and any reported subterfuge
like that could hurt Hamilberg's reputation. Bottom line — I
never saw Rooney at Hamilberg again.

It does happen, so any actor has to be sure that his legman isn't representing any possible competition to create a
conflict-of-interest situation.

Anyway, I became Jimmy Olsen, the young cub reporter
and photographer for the *Daily Planet*, in the movie serial
Superman vs. the Spider Lady. Kirk Alyn was Superman,
Noel Neill played Lois Lane, Pierre Watkins was Perry White,
and Carol Forman was the Spider Lady.

A serial consists of fifteen chapters, each twenty minutes
long — equal to three feature-length motion pictures. It was
shot over a period of one month. The work was just like making one long film. The dialogue followed the comic strip verbatim, even to the campy sayings, such as "Time is our mor-
tal enemy." Drop-shadow lettering was used for titles, stock
footage showed disasters, and space flight was by animation.
We used both a sound unit and a silent, or run-through, unit.
Spencer Bennett directed the sound unit, Tommy Carr the
silent. Carr was good at hacking out a serial. Bennett was
nice but nervous, and under a lot of pressure to keep within
Katzman's budget.

With the equivalent of three full-length motion pictures
to be made in a month, there was plenty of pressure. There
were three units working, one on the sound stage, one sound
unit on location, and a silent unit on location. I'd finish a
dialogue scene, and a car would whisk me to a run-through
on location. It might be a fight scence or something similar
over on Iverson's Ranch in Simi Valley, where lots of Westerns were made. Today the valley is covered with condos, but
in the forties, the area was covered only with boulders.

We shuttled back and forth, back and forth, until at the end of the day you didn't know whether you were coming or going. Really. In the studio, the scenes were shot out of sequence. We'd do scenes in Perry White's office, with Clark Kent, Lois Lane, and Jimmy Olsen. We would be working on a scene from page seven, then switch to a scene on page 400, and then back to page 200. One day we shot 103 scenes in Perry White's office, with dialogue. By 3 or 4 p.m. our minds had become such blanks we'd be writing dialogue on our hands. We shot scenes in White's office for three solid days, with everything out of context!

I appear in chapter one on a train with Lois Lane. We are reporting a mine disaster. Up ahead, the railroad track is cracked. Superman repairs the track and saves the racing train. When the engineer hits the brakes on seeing Superman up ahead, my typewriter falls into my lap. This was our first story about the Man of Steel. We meet Superman at the mine disaster and he saves Lois from a cave-in. And so on.

I performed many of my role stunts myself in *Superman.* I had a double who was dressed identically and did the difficult things, such as diving off a cliff. For closeups, where my face had to be visible, I had to learn stage fighting and how to roll downhill. The stunt men taught me a lot about their art.

My stunts were mostly confined to fighting where closeups were necessary. But there was one scene in which I was thrown onto a conveyor belt leading to a blast furnance. It was a real furnance, with real fire, not the crackling red cellophane used in the "Pirates of the Caribbean" ride in Disneyland. It was hot, and I could feel the heat, though I couldn't see the flames because I was being carried on my back, head first.

Tommy and Oliver Hardy look on as Stan Laurel punches Harry Woods who played Tommy's father in *Blockheads*, 1938. Courtesy of Larry Harmon Pictures Corp.

Edith Fellows is helping Tommy with his homework as Mary Gordon approves in *City Streets*, 1938. Courtesy of Columbia

Tommy doesn't seem pleased as Andy Clyde courts waitress Anita Garvin. Courtesy of Columbia Pictures.

The Five Little Peppers: Dorothy Ann Seese, Charles Peck, Edith Fellows, Bobby Larsen, and Tommy. Courtesy of Columbia Pictures.

Billy Gilbert straightens out troublemakers Butch and Buddy as Gloria Jean and Tommy approve in *A Little Bit of Heaven*, 1940. Courtesy of Universal Pictures.

Herbert Marshall pleads his case as a U.S. Senator in *Adventures in Washington*, as Tommy and other page boys observe. 1941. Courtesy of Columbia Pictures.

Jimmy Olsen (Tommy), Superman (Kirk Alyn), Lois Lane (Noel Neill), and Perry White (Pierre Watkins) listen for crucial information in Atom Man vs. Superman, 1948. Courtesy of D.C. Comics.

Jimmy, Lois, and Clark Kent in a mine in *Superman vs. the Spider Lady*, 1946. Courtesy of D.C. Comics.

Superman rescues Jimmy Olsen, in *Superman vs. the Spider Lady*, 1946.
Courtesy of D.C. Comics.

Celebrating with Perry White, Jimmy Olsen, Lois Lane, and Clark Kent. Courtesy of
D.C. Comics.

Noel Neill (Lois Lane), Tommy (Jimmy Olsen), and Kirk Alyn (Clark Kent—Superman) at their first reunion in over forty years. Anaheim Convention Center, Los Angeles, 1993.

Jimmy Lydon is drag racing with Tommy and their friends in *Hot Rod*, 1950.

A movie poster of *Gas House Kids in Hollywood*, 1947.

The Darling Sisters, Maryellen and Polly, performing for the troops during World War II.

Polly, her mother Norine Goebel, and her sister Maryellen, at Atlantic City during the Miss America Pageant, 1945.

Fredric March and Polly on the set of *Tomorrow the World*.

Tommy "Butch" Bond Jr. in a
publicity photo at twenty-one.

Being on the other side of the camera can be fun with David Frost and Jack Benny on *90 Minutes with David Frost*, 1972.

Tommy being inducted into *The Sons of the Desert* by Grand Sheik Bob Satterfield, 1985.

Tommy, Gordon "Porky" Lee, a fan, and George "Spanky" McFarland at a reunion in Palm Springs, 1986.

Our Gang reunion in 1980 in Los Angeles. *Back row, left to right:* William "Buckwheat" Thomas, Edith Fellows, Eugene "Pineapple" Jackson, Marvin Strend, Sid "The Woim" Kibrick, Joe Cobb, Ernie "Sunshine Sammy" Morrison, Leonard Landy, George "Spanky" McFarland, Tommy "Butch" Bond, and Delmar Watson. *Front row, left to right:* Dorothy "Echo" DeBorba, Verna Kornman, Peggy Ahern, and Mildred Kornman.

Tommy at the United
Cerebral Palsy Telethon in
Fresno, California, 1993.

Polly and Tommy in a
recent photograph.

The director had assured me: "Don't worry! We'll stop the conveyor before it reaches the furnace." He showed me his finger on a button that controlled the conveyor belt. "Trust me," he said when he showed me the button. But the belt kept moving. Closer, closer. When I was about two feet from the furnace and could feel the heat singing my head, I shot up, yelling: "Cut!, That's it! I'm not getting any closer to that thing!"

Unperturbed, the director said: "We were going to stop it." Sure.

Rusty Westcoat and his fellow stunt men, who helped teach me my stunts, told me many of their experiences. They doubled as actors in low-budget films. Sam Katzman kept a string of stunt men, a group of them for each picture. They might be pirates one week, gangsters the next, but, whatever their roles, they were the same skilled stunt men. They'd do anything — leap off buildings onto mattresses, knock each other around, jump into the sea, anything Sam asked.

The stuntmen did many things that are now done by special effects. When modern critics laugh at the effects in the 1946 *Superman*, they are displaying their ignorance. World War II had halted the development of special effects and it was not until after the war that the studios could concentrate on improving them. Though the first *Superman* series was made in 1946, it might as well have been made in 1940. It was tough to produce special effects in the absence of modern methods. The flying was pretty hokey in the 1946 *Superman*. To simulate take-off, Kirk Alyn ran, jumped and leaped over a camera on the ground. Then they cut to a wide shot, and the character was in animation, flying in a set position. Landing was simulated by Kirk as Superman jumping from a platform, or by the animated figure of Superman landing behind a car, followed by the real Kirk emerging from behind it.

The Katzmans heard criticism about Kirk Alyn not flying realistically. They found a better way when they made a follow-up to *Superman vs. the Spider Lady*. The first Superman serial was so successful that we made another, *Atom Man vs. Superman*, in 1948. It was released only to movie theaters and it was not until October 1993 that it premiered on AMC cable. The Atom Man was Lex Luthor, played by Lyle Talbot. He was as bald as Yul Brynner, because that's how Action Comics portrayed him. In this second serial, the Katzmans took a page from *Flash Gordon* (1936, 1938, 1940) and became the forerunner of Jerome Robbins' 1954 stage play *Peter Pan*, wherein Mary Martin flies via harness and track with the help of Peter Foy. In the 1948 *Atom Man vs. Superman*, Kirk wore a flying harness in front of a rear projection screen with fast-moving clouds going by and a wind machine blowing his hair back. The harness was attached to two guide wires, each with a control that moves him up and down or sideways. Today the various *Superman* movies are routinely shot with that method and chromakey, the use of colors that the film does not register. With appropriate lighting, a harness of such a color does not show.

Chromakey is an engineering marvel which television stations use. TV cameras have three tubes — red, blue, and green. A certain shade will be chosen (blue on NBC, green on ABC and CBS) and eliminated from the camera. If you're a weather announcer on ABC, for example, there's a green background, which is eliminated from the camera. The announcer can't wear green or he'll end up as a disembodied head and pair of hands. If the other two colors are used, he's in the picture. The map you see the weather announcer pointing to is actually a slide or a still. Shadows or ghost images are eliminated by the use of strong flat light. By this same process, your image can be projected onto any scene. You can appear to be flying over your city or the Grand Canyon.

During the 1980 get-together organized by the Sons of the Desert for old-time *Gang* members, I got almost as much recognition for *Superman* as for *Our Gang*. They were two highlights of my life on camera, but with a difference. *Our Gang* captured a period of American life that has disappeared. Maybe it was imaginative, but it portrayed childhood as people wanted to remember it. The *Superman* serials, on the other hand, are passé — vivid mostly in the recollections of movie buffs.

On the Golden Anniversary of Superman in 1988, fifty years after the comic strip started, reporters and ordinary people asked how it felt to have been in the original *Superman* film series. Let me tell you a bit about my co-stars, (and their successors in the George Reeves *Superman* TV series of the fifties and the Christopher Reeves *Superman* movies of the eighties).

After *Superman*, Kirk Alyn performed in movie serials. He was a good, hardworking actor. I don't know if he made other films. It might have been because he was typecast, I can't be sure. I did run into him in Knoxville, Tennessee, at a Superman revival in 1989. I also joined him and Noel Neill at a reunion in 1993. He still can't live it down! Kirk is now retired and living in Texas. Virginia O'Brien, who was his wife at that time, is still a good friend of mine. She was a good-looking brunette, a deadpan singer who worked in such MGM movies as *The Harvey Girls* and *DuBarry Was a Lady*.

George Reeves, who played a fine role as the TV Superman, was also typecast. After *Superman*, he couldn't find other work. He committed suicide. Christopher Reeves was an excellent Superman. He looked the part and his acting was marvelous.

Recognition has its price. I believe that those who have played Superman were stuck with the part, much as others were stuck with other series. Christopher Reeves, it seems, is the exception.

Noel Neill was at the Golden Anniversary of Superman and appeared with Jack Larson, who played Jimmy Olsen in the TV series. Phyllis Coates had played Lois Lane for a short time with George Reeves but, for some reason, she was replaced by Noel — the only one of the original characters to make it to the TV version. If you're not sure which one is Phyllis and which is Noel, well, Noel always wore the pillbox hat. Noel looked like Lois, tiny, five feet one inch, nice figure, and pretty face. It was wonderful joining her and Kirk at the 1993 reunion. Margot Kidder, who played Lois in the Christopher Reeves *Superman* movies showed wonderful acting ability.

Pierre Watkins was great as Perry White and even looked like Perry of the comic strips: white-haired, fast-talking, wisecracking, and cynical. He had dozens of movies to his credit when he went to work for the Katzmans. I was also with him in *Five Little Peppers*. Jackie Cooper played the role of Perry White in the Christopher Reeves movies.

A very nice touch, pointed out to me by a purist, was the use of Kirk Alyn and Noel Neill in a non-speaking scene in *Superman*, which stared Christopher Reeves. They were seated next to each other in the scene in which Clark Kent, the high school hero, races the train. It was nice to see the old and the new connected.

Purists love the 1946 and 1948 serials because they followed the Action Comics panels verbatim from Krypton's explosion. In the Action Comics and the serials, Superman's parents are high officials in the Krypton royal court. They try to warn the people to build a rocket fleet to escape an impending natural disaster. They do build a rocket and put their baby in it. It reaches Earth, and a farm couple retrieves the baby Superman from the rocket before it explodes.

The Christopher Reeves version followed the story of Superman's origins, but less closely. They needed a part for Marlon Brando, so they made him the father and gave him extra action, such as dispatching three evil characters who were not in the original story.

In the movies, Jimmy Olsen became a bit character, though *Superman IV* did give him more lines. I really don't know why they made him less important. In the comics, Jimmy was a major character, as he was on TV, always getting into trouble. Perhaps the movie producers wanted to emphasize the romance between Superman and Lois. Jimmy, therefore, wouldn't be important except as a foil.

Purist fans love the Jimmy Olsen role. A few years ago, Fresno County Superior Court Judge Stephen Henry, a man of great intelligence and accomplishments, visited the KFSN-TV studio where I was working, and came over to me.

"Oh, my God," he declared. "I've been wanting to meet you for the longest time."

"Why?"

"You were Jimmy Olsen. You were my idol!"

As I said, a man of great intelligence.

When TV Was A Novelty

Because of my movie roles I spread my studies at L.A. State College across three years, from 1948 to 1951, after spending two years at L.A. City. L.A. State (now California State University at L.A.) was founded in 1947 and for several years occupied bungalows on the L.A. City campus. It included a television department, and I felt lucky to enter this new department at a time when TV was in its infancy.

I was one of the first to buy a television set. It seemed like the ninth wonder of the world. Think of it! Transmitting pictures by air! At first the movie studios pooh-poohed it. They regarded it as a mere fad. How ironic that they had forgotten that only twenty years earlier the then-silent studios, in many cases headed by the same moguls, had similarly written off the use of sound. Well, thirty years later, the television studios would be pooh-poohing VCRs.

The technology for TV was created back in 1929, and it was a novelty at the 1939 World's Fair. However, the war interrupted its development. I had the highest respect for the engineers and the special effects they could produce. It was far beyond anything the motion pictures could do. At that time, however, few in the industry saw that far ahead.

Dr. Guardemal was my TV professor at L.A. State. He was formerly a drama teacher. We didn't have any TV equipment, so we took courses consisting of producing, acting, and directing. The courses were taught as a kind of mix between motion pictures and the stage. It was pretty much theoretical.

In making movies, scenes are shot out of sequence, but prior to videotape, TV was live. Shows like the old *Playhouse 90* required the actor to sustain a character throughout, much as in a stage play. So stage training came in very handy. Today soap operas are shot straight through, as in those days, but probably nothing else on videotape is done that way.

We needed equipment to make our department credible. "Tom, we have to find some kind of a TV outlet," Dr. Guardemal told me. I said that I'd check around. What I found was KHJ-TV on Vermont Street, near the campus.

KHJ was not California's first TV station. That honor belongs to KTLA, Los Angeles, which went on the air January 22, 1947, as Channel 5. KHJ began the following year, when two others, KNXT (now CBS) and KCOP also started.

KHJ was being struck by the American Federation of Television Artists (AFTA), the television actors' union, but I was able to go over there because the Screen Actors Guild (SAG), the actors' union to which I belonged, wasn't striking. I approached the program director and told him we had a college group putting on TV plays. He seemed interested, and when I asked if he'd want to air them, he said, "Sure." He checked with AFTA to make sure we wouldn't be blackballed as scabs.

The union had no objection because we were students. Once a week we went to KHJ and put on a performance.

Each week we rehearsed a thirty-minute drama or comedy in class, then went to the studio to rehearse a few more times. The director picked out the camera shots he wanted and we went for broke. It was live and non-stop, as all TV was in those days. I directed the actors, but I had nothing to do with giving camera directions at that time. If a mistake was made, no re-shooting was possible. Props were kept to a minimum. Scenery consisted of a black wall (the station invested nothing in scenery), and there were no costume changes because the story was kept to one scene.

The acting experience was valuable and the work with the big black-and-white cameras under the hot studio lights gave us a real taste of early TV.

I was graduated from L.A. State in 1951. Bill Webb, a buddy I'd known since high school, was a year ahead of me. He called and asked me what I planned to do.

"I dunno. Act, probably."

"Get smart," he advised. "Get on the other side of the camera."

"What do you mean?"

"In production, in TV," he said.

I considered his words. "If I knew someone, I might."

"Well," he announced, "I'm producing a show called *You Asked for It* with Art Baker, through Oxarart & Steffner." Bill worked as a producer for that agency.

Bill Webb was not alone in inducing me to go into TV production. Chuck Coon, KTTV's production manager, met with me after Bill arranged a no-guarantee job interview.

KTTV, originally affiliated with Dumont Broadcasting, was owned by the *Los Angeles Times*. It started broadcasting on Channel 11 on New Year's Day, 1949, and was the first station to be the TV arm of a newspaper. The *Times'* Norman

Chandler beat the *San Francisco Chronicle*'s KRON by eleven months, and the *Fresno Bee*'s KMJ (now KSEE) by four-and-a-half years. Obviously a growth industry.

KTTV was originally housed in the Bekins Building and then bought a new home at the Nassour Studios, on the corner of Sunset and Van Ness in Hollywood. That was a very good buy: seven acres of movie studios, four big stages, two large offices, and big sound stages with catwalks. All of this was easily converted to television production.

I met production manager Coon there. He was originally a set designer. When we first met, he was puffing on a pipe. He looked at me, and I could tell right away that he was a nice guy. After the initial pleasantries he got to the nitty-gritty.

"You want to go to work?"

"Sure." Why else would I be there? "What do I need?"

"Bring a hammer," he said.

"That's it?"

"That's it. You can start part-time on the night shift and weekends."

My mother was aghast when she heard that I was considering hiring on at KTTV. "You're not going to be a stage hand, are you?"

To her, production was a comedown from acting. I didn't agree. I had no desire to stay at home and wait for an agent to call with an occasional offer.

"Well," I assured her, "it's the only way to break into production. I love TV. I'm interested in it and want to be in the business. It's still young and, for me, a good start."

Against her wishes I took the job starting as a stage hand and began to put down professional roots. A stage hand puts up sets and, during a show, is responsible for any set movement. Later, I went on to set decorating and properties. The set decorator dresses the set with props, drapes, and so on;

the prop man assists him.

A big crew was needed during the age of live TV. One show would be shooting on one stage, while another was rehearsing on another stage. We'd shoot a half-hour live show here, then let the other show shoot, then we'd go back. It went on like that day and night. Station breaks were used for the switcheroos. There was no videotape and there were no re-takes.

There was a lot of hard work in early TV production. I had to be prop man, stage manager — everything. You had to learn all of it, and the pay was lousy — $62.50 for a 40-hour week. This was at a time when the movie production crews were earning ten times that amount. When KTTV leased sound stages to the movie studios, one of the set dressers, a good friend of mine, tried to convince me to go back to the movies. I shook my head. "No," I said. "There's security here, steady work fifty-two weeks a year, a paid vacation, and a health plan."

"But," he persisted, "look at the bucks you're not making."

"Yeah, well, I like the roots and the security here." I had been offered a chance to play Jimmy Olsen again when George Reeves' version of *Superman* was in the planning, and I turned it down. I was also offered the role of Hot Shot Charlie in *Terry and the Pirates*, and I turned that down, too, because by that time I had gone full-time at KTTV. (William Tracy got the part in *Terry*.) Later, some of the television stations absorbed some of the movie studios, former movie audiences were staying at home to watch free entertainment, and many of the fellows who had looked down on TV were out of work and came, hat in hand, to beg for the TV jobs they had once scorned. At KTTV, when the prop man's assistant left and a replacement was needed, I grabbed it and went full-time. More money, better hours, you understand. Eventually, I became head of the property department and stayed there while I was at KTTV. It was a good job, a prestigious job — the highest in the IATSE (International Alliance Theatrical and Stage Employees) union. But that came later.

When I started in production, doing a little bit of everything, I worked in a small studio, Studio F. It was used for movie matinees with a host such as Del Moore, Bill Leyden, Ed Reimers, or Sheriff John Rovik. The host delivered the commercials. Reimers was the "You're-in-good-hands-with-Allstate-Insurance" man. Sheriff John did a kiddie show. (His parting wish at each show was that you in the kiddie audience would "put another candle on your birthday cake.")

We had other kiddie shows, such as *Winchell-Mahoney Time*. Paul Winchell was a demanding, perfectionist type. I got into many fights while working with him. He used to make me nervous. I went to Jim Gates, the program director, and told him that either Winchell goes or I go. Well, not exactly like that. In fact, I told Gates, "I can't stand this guy any more. Get me off the show." The director merely responded, "Tom, when Paul Winchell is gone, you'll still be here."

The day before the one chosen for the cancellation of Winchell's show, Gates called me to his office and confided, "Now, you're the only one who knows this. Be on the set tomorrow at 10 a.m." When I asked what was going to happen, he informed me, "I'm going to call Mr. Winchell and tell him his show's been cancelled. I want you to see his reaction."

The next day I was the only one who knew, besides Gates, the head salesman, and the general director. I was on the stage when Winchell got a phone call on the set.

"Yes? Yes? Yes? Whaaat??"

He looked around and announced in a most astonished voice, "We've been cancelled!"

I summoned up all of my acting ability for an incredulous "No. . . . "

Winchell was a strange man. When my son was born he sent a savings bond and a box of candy. This surprised me since he had been so difficult to work with. He was a genius, having invented an artificial heart. About thirty years after that day in the studio I ran into him at Channel 30 when he was pitching his book on the artificial heart, and he was the friendliest man.

In many ways early TV really just televised radio. Most of the people in it had been in radio. We got them from network shows. Knox Manning (oddly enough, he did the opening narration on the original *Superman* serial) had done Nesbit's *The Passing Parade*, a radio show that became a TV show. George Burns and Gracie Allen, Jack Benny, and Bob Hope were all radio veterans. For those who had been in the movies, however, the transition was traumatic. Del Moore succeeded on Betty White's show, but he was one of the exceptions. For me, the transition to TV production was easy. I loved the work, and it was steady.

How did we broadcast live? Well, shows on the Dumont Network, such as Art Baker's *You Asked for It*, were broadcast by kinescope. The coaxial cable required for simultaneous network broadcasting coast to coast extended westward only to Omaha by 1950, and stations outside New York had to use kinescopes. The kinescope was a movie camera on a television tube that shot the show live. After the kinescope copy was made, it went right into the processor, unedited, and that's what the viewer got. We broadcast live to New York City at 4 p.m. Pacific time (7 p.m. Eastern time), and that was prime time. As it was being shot for New York it went into the processor for showing in Los Angeles at 9 p.m. It was the same show, only kinescoped. Like any live show, its disasters and unplanned funny spots couldn't be repaired.

Early TV had its share of screw-ups or bloopers with kinescope, but the audiences were tolerant, realizing it was live. No one thought anything of watching *Playhouse 90* and seeing someone get shot and then jump up, brush himself off, and walk away. Or the woman who had just shot her husband might open a door and find a stage hand standing there. Today, with edited tape, these things just wouldn't be seen.

My first show on KTTV was Art Baker's *You Asked for It.* The show was rehearsed all Sunday morning and then shot live at 4 p.m. The premise of the show was "Mrs. Cabbagepatch of Podunk, New York, you've asked to see whatever it is Podunkers like to see, and we're going to give it to you because You Asked for It." Sometimes, the audience at home got to see some bloopers. "Cannonball Smith" was one of these. It was rehearsed several times because of the many tricky camera shots. Cannonball's female assistant would light the fuse and he would catch the ball in his belly. At all the rehearsals, Baker announced the act, the assistant loaded the cannon and lit the fuse, drums rolled, the cannon fired, and Smith caught the ball with his belly. Perfect.

At 4 p.m., Art Baker announced: "Mrs. Stay-at-Home, you've always wanted to see a man catch a cannon ball with his stomach, and here it is. . . . " Load and light, rolling drums, loud boom . . . and the ball merely bounced forth gently. Undaunted, Smith rushed over, picked it up, and held it to his belly.

Jud Lederman, the special effects man at KTTV, was fascinated by explosives, but I don't believe he had a license. He did the setup for the "Indian Smoke Dancer" act. The Indian was supposed to dance around a stage filled with cut-out props of rock pedestals holding smoke pots that would blow up with flash powder. Jud had rigged up a master button and a control button wired for each pot. As the Indian danced around to the beating of drums, each pot would blow as he passed by. That was the act, and that's how it worked during rehearsals. Come the live production, however, Jud became so excited that he accidently hit the master button. All the pots blew at once. The dancer was burned and was so scared that he hid behind a cut-out mountain. That was the end of Jud Lederman's association with Art Baker.

Another time, two weeks were spent building a set to show Western stunt men fighting. A two-story saloon was erected with steps and balcony. Balsa wood tables, chairs, and a bar were built, and a candy-glass window was installed. The men were supposed to fight and break tables. A dance-hall girl behind the bar is married to one of the bad guys. The good guy pushes him to the bar and she reaches behind, picks up a bottle, breaks it over the good guy's head, and tosses him through the window into the street. There were five or six breakaway bottles right behind her, with real bottles on either side. Though they didn't break the window during rehearsal, it was beautiful in its rehearsed execution.

However, when the fight broke out during the live show, the dance-hall girl picked up one of the *real* bottles and k.o.'d the good guy. He slumped with a bump on his head and became dead weight. Realizing her mistake, she dragged his body to the window, picked him up, and threw him out. Anything for show biz.

There were some funny incidents connected with *You Asked for It* that never got on the stage. There was to be an elephant act, for example. The studio production head once walked out to the "alley" between sound stages where the trainer had his elephant. The trainer was chanting and moving around in a strange dance which the pachyderm imitated. The production head was curious.

"Is that some kind of ritual you're doing with the elephant?"

"No," came the reply, "that's how I make him shit."

Commercials could provide some humorous moments on-and-off camera. The commercials were as live as the shows they sponsored.

One wasn't so funny at the time because it almost got me fired. *The Dude Martin Show* on KTTV in 1952 was a Western-type song-and-comedy show. Hank Penny, whose trademark song was "Won't You Ride in My Little Red Wagon?" wanted a gag to make a furnace spew out black smoke. I loaded a vacuum cleaner with cocoa to reverse-blow the imitation smoke. Unaware of the consequences, Hank lit the cocoa, it exploded, and he was singed. I saved my job by showing the boss what happens to cocoa powder when set afire.

Ted Linz, an advertiser, was doing a commercial on Bill Leyden's show. He came to me one day and said, "Tom, I'm doing a commercial tomorrow on a beer tapper. Here's a full keg and here are two Pilsner glasses. Set it up, and I'll walk in and ask 'How would you like to have a cold glass of beer?' I'll draw a glass and toast the audience at home."

He wanted the pony keg locked up for the night and wheeled in for the 1 p.m. show. No problem. I told my assistant about it and went about my business.

The next day Ted came in, asked if everything was ready, found out it was, and said, "Great, let's go live."

"How would you like to have a cold glass of beer?" He turned, pulled the tap, and pssss — empty!

All hell broke loose in the commercial operations section. Later they discovered that one of the night security guards had single-handedly finished the entire pony keg.

I could work anywhere I wished after I put in my contractual forty hours a week at KTTV. I could work with any other studio or station. I took a spin at the local CBS (now KCBS) studio.

A visual special effect I worked on at CBS in the mid-1960s was with Pat Paulsen, turning him into the Wolfman on the Glen Campbell Show. Paulsen was the man who ran for President on a shoestring budget in each election from 1968 through 1992. There was a live audience that saw the entire process in stop-frame, of course, but the viewers at home saw only the transformation of the Caspar Milquetoast Pat Paulsen into one of the most ferocious mythological beasts.

Pat was rocking in a chair on his porch, singing "Blue Moon," with a brace on the back of his neck to hold his head steady. Suddenly he stopped singing and the camera stopped taping. A makeup man rushed up and applied makeup. The makeup man left and the taping and singing resumed. The taping stopped, more makeup was applied, the taping was resumed, and so on. At the end of this tedious process, Paulsen rose as the Wolfman, howled and chased a girl off the stage. He had to freeze while waiting during each makeup pause, and this displayed pure genius (with an assist from the neck brace). If you saw the movie, *American Werewolf in London* (Universal, 1981), this is how the young fellow was transformed.

Sounds, another type of special effect, are made backstage, otherwise microphones would have to be placed all over the set. Walking, slamming doors, gunfire — are all done off-stage. On radio they did it with fake sounds — using tin for thunder, miniature doors, coconut halves for galloping horses, and crumpled cellophane for fire. It's all illusion, and I loved being a part of it.

In 1963 the *Los Angeles Times* sold KTTV to Metromedia and, without changing its call letters, Channel 11 became part of Metromedia Television. I stayed with it until the end of 1972, twenty years with the same employer. This was a record for me. I had made the right move, despite my mother's chagrin and my set dresser friend's disbelief. Between 1975 and 1991, I worked with KFSN-TV in Fresno. When I moved to KFSN I worked with Al Case in advertising. Al liked my L.A. background and experience. We had our share of funny experiences, though in retrospect, they're funnier now.

Commercials certainly employ special effects because sometimes reality just can't be captured. I remember Maxwell Coffee once sponsored a spot on KTTV. The sponsor wanted to show a steaming cup of coffee. No problem, you think. Except that steam rising is very difficult to shoot, even with a black background. A special effects friend from the movies advised me to use liquid smoke. Liquid smoke is not the same substance you'll find on your supermarket spice rack as a flavor enhancer. It's obtainable only from a special effects house and can be very toxic. Once the cork is popped, it begins to work.

My friend told me to take some out of the bottle with an eyedropper, put one or two drops on the saucer behind the cup and then recap the bottle. I was busy with a million other things, so I told one of the station prop men what to do.

He forgot.

He poured out a spoonful. Smoke billowed all over. He couldn't see where the cup was. The stage had to be cleared, and blowers had to be turned on to get rid of the toxic smoke.

Television-viewing consumers are often fooled by food ads. Chicken may be painted brown, and liquid soap put in coffee to make bubbles.

The neatest commercial trick I ever saw was performed by a prop man for "Brew 102." How do you get a perfect head on a glass of beer? First he added a pinch of salt, then placed a light under the glass to show the beautiful color.

145

From this I learned how to make snow on a stage for Channel 11 without using a snow shaker. Snow shakers are of limited use. They're twelve-feet-wide placards, moved back and forth to drop the plastic snow. A stage would require two or three of them.

I bought a tall, narrow aquarium, filled it with the contents of three cases of the cheapest beer, and added a pinch of salt. I covered the back of the aquarium with black paper, and then cross-lit it. By using the reverse sweep on the old black-and-white cameras (turning the picture upside down), the bubbles became falling snow. This was used for Christmas openings and similar shots, and later was preserved on video tape.

Other special effect commercials I worked on at KTTV were for Gallo Wines, with Paul Henreid of *Casablanca* fame, in black-and-white, and a local product, Fredelis Frozen Dinners, using Hal Smith.

Smith has had a long career in films. He played the drunk on the *Andy Griffith Show*. Fredelis Frozen wanted Smith, nicknamed "Freddie Fredelis," to jump down the shelves of a refrigerator.

There was no chromakey in those days, but there was a grey key. We keyed in grey, shot him leaping off a grey platform with a grey wall background. By eliminating the grey and reducing, we made him teeny-tiny and superimposed him over the refrigerator. Such are Filmland's amazing tricks.

Polly

Like most red-blooded males I enjoyed looking at pretty girls. Always did. But until my mid-twenties, the feminine half of the world really didn't play an important part in my life.

It might surprise you that I didn't date movie actresses. I knew many of course, girls like Shirley Temple, but I preferred non-actresses. In high school I wanted to be "one of the gang," and those "regular" girls were the type I dated. There were never serious relationships because the war and my certain involvement in it militated against any kind of honorable commitment.

When I got out of the Navy and went to *Superman* I avoided the female extras like the plague. Many were opportunistic gold-diggers — befriending people to get into the movies. A lot of them were a new type of girl. They expected tough give-and-take, not flowers and candy in the way I had been raised to treat women.

So what did I do for a social life? I played canasta.

My friend Bill Webb was married. Our friends Dave and Natalie owned a home in Laguna. Bill Stillwalt, Sherry Hall, and I would invite female drama students we knew. We'd pool what little money we had to buy eggs for the next morning's omelettes and spend Friday night swimming and playing canasta. It was more like a club than anything else.

I used to wonder if anything was wrong with me. Why hadn't I met the right girl? Was she out there? Were my standards impossibly high? Yes and no. Well, it wasn't time.

Then along came Polly!

There's a scene in chapter twenty of Mario Puzo's *The Godfather* where Michael, in Sicilian exile, sees Apollonia and is hit with "the thunderbolt." He will have her for his wife. No ifs, ands, or buts. Well, Polly sparked my thunderbolt.

There were parallels in our lives that went back before the turn of the century. Both of our maternal grandfathers had worked for the railroad (when they eventually met, they could swap tall ones about the James boys and others they'd encountered). Her father and my mother were born about a block apart, yet Polly and I had no knowledge of each other until the day we met.

Pauline Francis Goebel was born in Houston on July 20, 1928, the daughter of William Goebel and the former Norine Ellis. Her mother's family came over on the *Mayflower*. Their descendants settled in Kansas City, Missouri, where her uncle married into the Pendergast family that ran Missouri politics and gave Harry Truman his start.

Like me, Polly had a slightly older sister, Mary Ellen. And, like me, she was a child of the Depression. Their country club membership was dropped, her family's bank accounts disappeared, and she learned to enjoy the simple things in life — such as turning a Quaker Oatmeal box into a dozen different toys.

The South was forty years behind the rest of Western civilization as far as equal rights and opportunities for the sexes were concerned, so Polly and Mary Ellen were raised to be "girls." Their upbringing was strict, with Sundays centered around the Lutheran church. It was expected that they would marry and, if they had to work, the only professions that they could enter honorably were teaching or nursing. That's the way it was in those days.

Like most middle-class children, the sisters were given singing and dancing lessons. Polly loved to sing and dance and was drawn to show business. While other kids, including her sister, skated and biked, she made up stories and songs and performed before a mirror.

Eventually her dad got his business back on track and things grew better. In 1940, when Polly was twelve, her music teacher told their mother that Polly and Mary Ellen were ready for professional work. Beautiful voices apparently ran in the Goebel family (one of their uncles had been a radio crooner). The music teacher sent them to a friend, a theatrical booking agent, who asked the girls to sing a duet. They chose a Western song, "Goodbye, Little Darlin'." The agent liked their projection and booked them in Galveston, Texas, for the weekend.

With several army training centers nearby, there was a built-in audience. The two girls were good. They did five shows on Saturday and four on Sunday, opening with "Goodbye, Little Darlin'" and then relying on solos, for they didn't have any other duets. On Monday morning it was back to school.

The sisters had gone to a Lutheran school and then transfered to St. Agnes Academy, a Catholic girls' school. The nuns were helpful and cooperative, taking an interest in their musical careers and offering to permit them an occasional Monday off if their school work was completed. Their own Lutheran church, however, was aghast at the girls' going into show business and refused communion to their parents, causing a great deal of heartache and soul searching.

Out of the soul searching came Mrs. Goebel's determination to see that her daughters got the careers they wanted. Polly has remarked that, if her independent-thinking mother had been around during the bloomer days, she too would have worn bloomers, like the pioneer Mrs. Amelia Bloomer. The girls' dad was somewhat more conventional, but their mother usually prevailed.

Polly and Mary Ellen were too young for USO shows, but their act was chosen for one of the many bond drives in the Southwest. Their mother drove them from town to town. They'd hit a town, rehearse with a new pick-up band (very often men who were unable to read the music), put on the show, and drive on to the next scheduled destination. The driving presented a problem, since gasoline was rationed. They weren't privileged card-holders even though they were entertaining to keep up war-time morale. Trains were almost entirely commandeered for military use. The tour was a lot of fun despite all the inconveniences.

Polly, Mary Ellen, and their mother had lived sheltered lives. While improving her show-business know-how, Polly also learned something about the real world. In Palacios, Texas, near Corpus Christi, for example, there was a boarding house next door to the theater where they performed. The drummer in the program that accompanied their act had been with Gene Krupa. Once, in the middle of the night, he began to beat the drums and shout crazily. Polly's mother read the Bible to him and he calmed down.

Even though the girls were minors and not supposed to play in nightclubs, still they did. Respecting the innocence of Polly and Mary Ellen, the chorus members never uttered profanities around them.

Mary Ellen was graduated from high school in 1943, Polly in 1945. Soon after graduating, Mary Ellen married a serviceman who went overseas.

In the summer of 1944 they met a 20th Century-Fox talent scout who was judging a beauty contest. He liked the girls and thought they had enough talent to be included in a forthcoming Betty Grable musical.

Polly, Mary Ellen, their mother, their Pekinese dog, and the talent scout (who did the driving) set out for Hollywood from Houston. They drove straight through along old Route 66 to meet a studio deadline.

Mary Ellen couldn't sign a contract because the law at that time would not allow a woman to enter into one without her husband's consent or in the absence of his power of attorney. Polly didn't have that problem, and she was signed to a seven-year contract with options. That's the studio's options, remember. It was a typical slavery, excuse me, stock contract.

At 20th Century she had tutors to rid her of her Texas twang and to give her more lessons in singing and dancing. She was given a chance to read for any secondary parts that opened up.

She also had to date stockholders. Most of the studios in those days required this of the young starlets. But Polly, having her own set of morals, refused to be told what to do and with whom. She didn't drink or smoke, but preferred spending her money on clothes and cosmetics rather than tobacco. At Hollywood parties she put her filled champagne glass under her chair. Occasionally Polly experienced harrassment with threats of not having her contract renewed, yet she maintained her moral values.

She never did play in a 20th Century movie.

Another thing that Polly and I had in common was the same agent, P.B. Mahoney. Remember P.B.? He was the one who brought me out to meet Mr. Roach, and he was Polly's agent in Hollywood.

Polly's career wasn't going anywhere. P.B. was angry at the studios for wasting such a talent and suggested that she enter a beauty pageant to give her career a boost. Polly had a winning personality and won the first round to enter the Miss California Pageant. In those days girls were not selected as Miss County or Miss Locality. They came from all over the state to compete for the Miss California title.

The contest was held at the Aragon Ballroom in Ocean Park, California. Three hundred beautiful girls from small towns and big cities descended on Ocean Park.

The 300 were narrowed down to 32. Polly's father meantime had moved to Southern California and had taken a job with Hughes aircraft. It was he who encouraged and trained her. She walked three or four miles a day to keep her figure in shape. There was a final appearance of the thirty-two girls in two sections, a final-final with five, and a last winnowing. She thought she'd fail because of her height, five feet two inches, but the judges — Rudy Vallee, the King Brothers, Olympic skating champ Belita, and a dress designer — chose her. Polly Ellis (using her mother's maiden name because she was underage) became Miss California of 1945!

There were two runners-up. They were given the titles of Miss Hollywood and Miss San Diego. As Miss California, Polly was entitled to a wardrobe, money, a glamour girl movie part, and train tickets to Atlantic City, New Jersey, home of the Miss America Pageant since 1921.

One of the partners in the Aragon Ballroom was colloquially known as "Mr. Big." Miss San Diego was his girlfriend. Naturally, he expected her to win the state title. When she didn't, he was not only disappointed, he was angry. Someone pointed out the fine print in the Miss America rules which permitted a contestant to enter as a Miss City, so he decided that Miss San Diego would go to Atlantic City to compete for the big title. Polly's feisty mother was determined that her daughter would not be mistreated and purchased train tickets for herself and Mary Ellen to go along with Polly.

"Mr. Big" ran around with a rough bunch, and Polly received a warning that if she went through with plans to go East, she'd be "met" in Chicago. In those days Chicago was still famous for its criminal underworld, and to many people in many lands "Chicagogangster" was one word. It was with this warning that Polly, Mary Ellen, and their mother boarded the Pullman car on the Santa Fe Chief.

At each stop the porter announced: "Miss California is coming out for her stroll." All of the servicemen on the train would jump off to assemble on the platform to watch her walk, accompanied by her ladies and the porter.

In Chicago they had to cross town to switch to the Broadway Limited at another railroad station. Somewhat fearful, they decided to wait until the Santa Fe Chief emptied, so that they might sneak off.

Up came a man in a fedora. (Have you seen *The Untouchables*?) "Are you Miss California?"

Butterflies in the belly.

"I'm from the *Sun*."

How do you spell relief?

On to Philadelphia where they were met by the owner of

the Philadelphia Phillies. Polly's dad was quite a baseball fan, so the team owner obligingly gave them some mementos for him and escorted them to Independence Hall and other historic sites. They then took the ferry across the Delaware and the train from Camden to Atlantic City.

During the Miss America Pageant, each contestant was assigned an official hostess, or shared one, in addition to her own chaperones. In Polly's case her mother and sister were her chaperones, and she shared an official hostess with Miss New Orleans, a hep gal from Basin Street.

The Chicago-type threats began to materialize on the second day of the pageant. There was heavy betting on the outcome of the pageant, as on a horse race or boxing match. There was a good deal at stake, and there were inevitable moves to put some contestants out of the running by intimidation. Then, on the second day, Polly's hostess begged off for the evening while two goons made their way to the floor where Polly and Miss New Orleans were staying. The goons were waiting for her. Just before Polly arrived, Mary Ellen and Miss New Orleans' chaperone came off the elevator, noticed the goons, and swiftly walked toward them. The goons fled, and a complaint brought a police guard, who remained on duty for the rest of the pageant.

The Miss America Pageant had four basic contests: bathing suit, talent, evening dress, and speaking. Polly was winning in each category, so the press started to treat Polly as the winner. The day before the coronation the newsreel reporters and photographers told her that their count of the judges' points made her the winner, and they wanted to get footage of her with the audience applause. "Act like she's just been crowned," they told the audience.

"Mr. Big" flew to Atlantic City on the final day. He politely informed Polly's mother that "our little girl has gone far enough." However, if her mother would sign a contract giving him control of Polly's career, amounting to a kind of adoption, then she might wear the crown. Her mother told him to get lost. Thereupon, "Mr. Big" proceeded to get Polly disqualified for being under age. Most women would lie about their ages — my future wife had to be different.

So who got the title? Bess Myerson, Miss New York.

The reaction? Pandemonium. The audience threw bottles onto the stage, hooted and otherwise showed their displeasure. The emcee, Bob Russell, came backstage with tears in his eyes.

"You know," he said, "this breaks my heart. You got a raw deal here. Listen to the people. They know."

He quit the pageant.

There were ripples among the other contestants. Naturally, they hadn't liked Polly when she was winning, but now they were outraged by the injustice and promised to talk to their local chambers of commerce.

Notoriety or fallout from the pageant did nothing to harm Polly's career. Howard Hughes wanted her to come to New York so that he might sponsor her career as an actress, but she couldn't go. She had agreed to become an understudy at Universal Studios.

So, to Universal. Sue Carroll's agency took Polly as a client. Sue was Alan Ladd's wife and had made him a star. Sue sent Polly to Paramount, and then from Paramount she went to Selznick, whose vice-president had young, promising stars like Rock Hudson.

Polly switched from Sue Carroll to MCA. When movies didn't pan out for her she became a photographer's model for Tom Kelly and her pictures appeared in *Vogue* and *Catalina*.

She posed for ads for such disparate products as orange juice and beer.

One of the first KTTV kiddie shows was *Range Rider* in which Polly and Mary Ellen, known as the "Darling Sisters," sang Western songs. It was difficult to get into live TV, but for those with vaudeville training it was a little easier. They had it, so they made it.

Polly and Mary Ellen started the first Toys for Tots drive at Grauman's Chinese Theater. They brought out George Jessel, Gorgeous George, and Gregory Peck. Peck's two young sons were fans of *Range Rider.* They wouldn't let their father go home until he got Polly's and Mary Ellen's autographs. Kids in those days felt a personal relationship with TV performers.

The "Darling Sisters" sang on Jimmy Wakely's and Ray "Crash" Corrigan's shows, and appeared in Bob Lippert's movie *Variety Show* which incorporated all types of Hollywood variety acts.

The sisters didn't confine themselves to TV singing. They cut Western records for the Crystal Recording Company. You had to be sharp in that business.

From the beginning, Mary Ellen had not been deeply interested in the work. Her goal was marriage and motherhood and she had married. When she became pregnant she retired. Polly, having always worked together with her sister as a duo, went solo with some trepidation.

Polly had married a civil engineer in 1949, but the marriage didn't work out. He was a nice fellow, but they found they weren't compatible and they divorced in 1950. The newspapers made something of her divorce, considering her prominence as a singer. However, I hadn't noticed and was not aware of the marriage until I met her.

Polly was hurt by the experience, and after her divorce she became turned off to men. She became career-minded and avoided distractions. Least of all she wanted an actor-husband. She regarded actors as unstable and self-centered.

Her first solo job after her sister retired was on the first L.A. nighttime show to run live commercials between movie showings. Across the street was the Hollywood Ranch Market. The Goodwin advertising agency employees were always going there and bringing back doughnuts and other goodies. They offered them to Polly, but she was on a diet. A staff relief announcer used to come in early and tell her some of the night's jokes before show time. Then he'd give her a hungry look.

"I'm not going to eat these doughnuts," Polly would say, and he would ask, "May I have them?"

"Please take them," she'd respond. "You're doing me a favor."

The young man was Johnny Carson.

After six months at KTTV, I happened to be the assistant director of the show that advertised Corrigan's Ranch. Polly had been a guest on the show a couple of times, but I hadn't seen her before. Guitar in hand, Polly was to do a love song with a young singer on the *Charlie Aldridge Country-Western Show*, in which he played the guitar and acted. All live, remember.

When she arrived at the studio, Polly asked me to hand her guitar to her ever-present mother. I did, and it was a lucky thing for me. Let me tell you, get the mother's approval and you're nearly home.

Polly was performing in her leather cowgirl outfit. Her mother sat by, watching the monitor to be able to offer criticism later. I was standing near her mother, holding the guitar, and also watching.

And then it happened. I looked at Polly. Our eyes met. Electricity flowed. And I did the smart thing — I started talking to her mother. We talked about common roots, Texas, and so on. After Polly's scene, I handed her the guitar. We talked of various and sundry things. She was unaware that I had been an actor (she had never paid much attention to the *Gang*), and she invited me over to swim. I got her phone number and made a date to take her to Nick O'Dell's restaurant on Melrose. That's where the movie and TV crowd went for lunch — and still do — to save a few pennies as compared with the Brown Derby.

On our first date I ordered my all-time, everlasting favorite, steak and tomatoes. But neither of us ate our dinners, so there must have been something there. We held hands and then I took her home.

We talked a few more times. She was a fascinating conversationalist. A pattern developed — daily calls and weekly weekend dates. It was as if I'd known her all my life. We both had show-business careers and we knew the drawbacks of show-biz marriages. But after six months of dating I summoned up the courage to propose. I don't think a man can be braver than that. Even going into combat pales before it. You put your whole life in your offer to another human being. Her response can determine the course your life will follow. At that moment she has the power to bring you heavenly delight or to cast you into emotional hell.

What did she say? Not much. She didn't want to be hurt again, naturally, and I promised not to hurt her. I meant it. But did she say "yes"? No, not yet.

When I proposed the first time I guess she must have reacted: "What a jerk." But I persisted. "Wear 'em down" was my motto. Apparently it was my faithful daily call that did it, for she finally said "yes"!!!!

Both our families were delighted. A big June wedding was planned.

On our weekly date, on April 18, 1952, we had a couple of martinis with Chinese food. I looked at her and asked, "Do you really want to wait until June?"

She: "What do you mean?"

Me: "Let's drive to Vegas and do it."

It's 300 miles from Los Angeles to Las Vegas. That's six hours via San Bernardino, Barstow, and Baker. But to a man in love, what's that? She agreed, and we drove through the evening and into the night, with only the clothes on our backs. We arrived in Vegas at 11 p.m. And then she threw a curve.

"I'm a Lutheran," she reminded me. "We have to be married in a Lutheran chapel."

If she thought that was a roadblock, she was wrong. "I'll find one," I assured her.

At the Clark County Courthouse — open all night for crazies like us — we got our papers and, upon inquiring, were told there was a chapel down the street staffed by a Lutheran minister.

But now she was getting cold feet. I was reassuring her that I didn't want to rush her, when out she blurted — "We'll do it!"

"Let's go." I wasn't taking any chances.

At 2 a.m. (actually on the 19th, though our papers said the 18th), a fully garbed Lutheran minister answered our knock on the chapel door. We assured him we had the license. He offered a package deal with a professional weeper, a professional rice thrower, a few tin cans tied to the bumper of my car and a "Just Married" sign for the back window, probably from a professional car decorator.

And so, as the Bible says, we became "one flesh."

We had no motel reservations and our families didn't know our whereabouts, but we were now married. What next?

We went to eat and have a few drinks at the Thunderbird restaurant, with its huge glass window overlooking the desert. Trying to unwind at 4 a.m. we were startled by a big flash of light over Yucca Flats — like a movie arc light, only whiter.

One of the men at the next table remarked, "Boy, it's the biggest one we've ever seen!"

What was he talking about? "Biggest what?" I asked.

"Why an atomic bomb!"

We had another drink, then headed for a motel. Before retiring we called our parents and let them know. They weren't overjoyed to miss a big June wedding but had to accept that what was done was done. The next day Polly and I drove back to L.A.

Polly had always been very close to her family. Texas people are very family-oriented, and I liked her folks. It was almost like having a second set of parents. As a family, we've lived together ever since — through happy times and sad — moving first to Remington Avenue, in the north San Fernando Valley, then to Studio City, Sherman Oaks, Dunlap, Fresno and Madera — all in California.

A Family Man

When we returned from our jaunt across the desert, Polly went on Bob Davis's show. He didn't think our marriage would last, nor did most of the other Hollywood people who knew us. Davis, her co-star, teased me with "You lucky bum" and "That's OK, I'm patient," and then he would sing, "I'm walking behind you on your wedding day." My friend, floor director Bill Steirwalt, seeing me come to lunch with Polly every day (and probably figuring I was a hopeless case), put me in charge of the show she was in. Many others at the studio made bets on our marriage, giving me maybe six weeks. Well, we celebrated our fortieth anniversary in 1993.

In a decision that many career women today might not understand, Polly didn't go on the road with Charlie Aldridge, nor did she take up an excellent offer for a new Western series. Until then the only actress in Westerns was Dale Evans. Polly was offered a chance in this new series, which the producer thought might run two or three years. Unfortunately, three or four months on location in Arizona were part of the package, and, as a newlywed, she decided to turn it down. Further, she decided that ours would be a one-career household.

The part? It was Miss Kitty in *Gunsmoke*.

For years, Polly teased me about that, as our marriage and *Gunsmoke* went on and on.

But Polly's film career wasn't quite over. She played in *Divorce Court*, a TV series produced by one of my friends, Jackson Hill, in which the judge and litigants were actors but the attorneys were genuine and unrehearsed. *Divorce Court* used the Boleslavsky technique of improvisation. The actors were given certain details of their particular situation and had to wing it from there.

My mother was a Presbyterian, but I was never much of a churchgoer. After I was married, Polly wanted me to go to church with her, so, with her gentle persuasion, I was baptized and confirmed in the Lutheran Church.

It was as a member of Emmanuel Lutheran Church of North Hollywood that Polly resumed her acting career in 1957. The pastor of Emmanuel Lutheran and his wife, Marge Wold, were wonderful people.

I had an idea to stage a Christmas pageant, and along with Polly and the help and skills of many others, we carried it out. It lasted for eleven years, from 1957 to 1968. Even KTTV was impressed and broadcast the pageant without commercials.

Polly worked with me in producing two Christian dramas penned by Marge Wold, *Penny for a Sparrow* and *Purple Sackcloth*. Aside from those, her acting career was over.

I helped in the production of Father Bud Kaiser's *Insight*, a weekly half-hour drama on KTTV. Kaiser, a Catholic priest, had no show-business background, but he had a dream: to dramatize the triumph of good over evil. From 1960 to 1983 he created about 150 episodes through Paulist Productions in L.A. My challenge was to decorate sets, and I roamed from prop store to prop store in my search.

Insight gave me a chance to work with real professionals. There were great writers like John Furia, directors like Jack Shea, and actors like Ricardo Montalban and Brian Keith. Who knows how the work helped other people?

What about the rest of my family?

My grandma died in 1952, just after I met Polly. Polly, in fact, scared me a little by reading my palm on our first date, telling me that someone very dear to me was going to die. A week later it came true. I missed my grandmother, for she had been the strong woman during my childhood.

Dad stayed in commercial art until age made his hands unsteady. He began to go downhill, probably from Alzheimer's disease, though we can't be sure. He died in Veterans Hospital in the San Fernando Valley in 1971.

We then tried to encourage Mom to move to our Dunlap Ranch, but she was an independent sort, although not really a loner. She prefered living alone and going to her church services and her bridge parties. In 1972, a month after I last saw her, she passed away from a heart attack.

My sister Jane and her second husband lived in Southern

California where she was an artist and sculptor. She passed away in 1991. My father-in-law died at Dunlap in 1975. My mother-in-law passed away in Madera in 1988.

In 1970, I was working 'round the clock at the studio, or so it seemed. I'd do my regular work, then *Soul Train* wanted me on the weekend, along with the other shows which couldn't shoot without me. It was great to be wanted and appreciated, but enough was enough. The family wasn't seeing me. I wasn't even seeing myself. Polly got fed up with the situation and, typically, resolved to solve it. Her solution — a getaway spot.

She subscribed to the United Farm Catalog which listed farms and ranches for sale. The catalog advertised "little cabin in the mountains on six-and-one-half acres with a lazy stream going by." It was situated in Dunlap, a town of 600 people, 40 miles east of Fresno.

Polly liked it. We bought it and used it for weekend retreats. On Friday afternoons, we piled into the car and headed for the hills, arriving by 10 p.m. We spent Saturdays there and came home Sunday afternoon. It made for a pleasant weekend.

Polly's mother had an idea of raising cattle for profit.

The same catalog that brought us to Dunlap advertised another larger place on Dunlap Road, 130 acres with a house, three outbuildings and a three-quarter mile of stream.

We took a tour and couldn't believe there was so much land available. We were all eager to move there so, in 1973, we sold the small ranch and Polly's mother sold her house and we moved lock, stock, and barrel to the big ranch in Dunlap.

I quit KTTV. I never planned to go back to television. Like the *Gang*, like the movies, like radio, it was a closed chapter. Or so I thought.

My plan was to raise cattle with my nephew Corky. I wanted to raise my own corn for feed and get a job to pay the bills until the cattle started to turn a profit.

A ranch presents economic problems. To stay in ranching one should have a second income. During the year after I took off from KTTV I had lots of time to think about the future. I loved the time off, but I needed a steady income. So I began to commute to L.A.

For about ten years while at KTTV I had been moonlighting for Hughes Sports Network, coordinating their sporting events on weekends. As coordinator, my job was to go to the home base station that aired the game and also ran the commercials. There I had to screen the commercials prior to airing, to make sure they were in order and would be properly aired. Hughes flew me to San Francisco, Portland, and Seattle to cover games. When I left KTTV, I kept my finger in that pie.

A good thing, too. When the ranch didn't work out I took a spot with Hughes. It helped make ends meet. But it just wasn't enough.

I also kept my membership in Local 33 of the I.A.T.S.E., the theatrical stage hands' union in Los Angeles. The union kept a call system whereby if you wanted one or two weeks' worth at a network, they'd get you on. I started doing that and put my application in at the three network stations in Fresno: KMJ, Channel 24, (now KSEE, formerly owned by the Fresno *Bee* and affiliated with NBC); KFSN, Channel 30, (owned by Capital Cities, formerly affiliated with CBS, now with ABC); and KJEO, Channel 47, (owned by Retlaw, formerly affiliated with ABC, now CBS).

Some of you may think it was foolish to give up a sure thing with KTTV. After all, I'd been there more than twenty years. Well, you know what they say are the only two certainties in this world. Metromedia, the company that had been touted as the fourth network, sold KTTV to Fox Broadcasting, and Fox laid off three-fourths of its workers. So, I think I made the right move at the right time.

While I would have been happy to be hired by any of the Fresno stations, I really wanted to work for Channel 30. Capital Cities was a growing operation, with new buildings and studios. It bought ABC. In short, Channel 30 was the Cadillac of Fresno broadcasting. I never thought I'd be hired by 30, but I was in 1975.

It was only part-time, a bitter pill to swallow after twenty-three years in the business. But it was very tough to break into local TV. Lee Jason, the program director, called Polly and announced, "I got Tommy's foot in the door, but that's all I can promise."

I stayed at 30 and eventually went full-time.

What did I do there? I was an assistant director responsible for news shows, talent, and all location productions for commercials. I was also in charge of all the stages. Compared to KTTV, KFSN was a smaller station, so I wore several hats. For example, I was in charge of incoming merchandise and commercial props and called painters and carpenters under my control when we needed sets built. I also ran chyron, the character generator that identified at the bottom of the TV screen who was being interviewed during a news report.

At KFSN two instances of commercial special effects stand out in my mind. One involved a fog machine for General Electric and the other, the famous Dancing Raisins.

Five minutes of fog could be manufactured by using a fifty gallon barrel with a hot water coil welded into it. Fill with water, then heat, add dry ice, and, with only a little pipe coming from the barrel, you could make a good fog, especially if the barrel is covered.

The Dancing Raisins were about three or four inches high. The assignment was to make them come up through a mound of real raisins. Al Case, the producer, and I got our heads together. Five sona tubes (cardboard tubing) of various lengths were painted raisin color, and attached to a half-inch of foam board. The wall behind was green chromakey. The dancers came up through the sona tubes as we raised the platform. The raisins themselves were quite sticky, but we put cocoa powder on them to reduce the stickiness. All of that for a ten-second spot.

Going to Channel 30 didn't end our Dunlap lives. We were there for another ten years, and it had some influence on what my son did in show biz.

15

Butch, Jr.

From the late forties into the fifties, couples were having babies soon after marriage. A doctor told Polly that because of various problems she would probably never have a child. There's a disappointment at such news, but one accepts and goes on. Anyway, I had my lovely wife, and as long as she was fine, I'd be happy. After all, I'd married her for herself. Eleven years of blissful marriage rolled on. And then it happened!

In October, 1963, Polly became pregnant. Medical science had advanced during the previous decade, and the obstetrician assured us that everything would be fine.

After ten months, on August 12, 1964, in Encino, Polly was delivered of an eight-pound, seven-ounce baby boy. We named him Thomas R. Bond II, but he quickly succeeded to my old moniker, Butch.

At the age of seven, our second-grader was getting into trouble in school and bringing home bad grades. Since we were concerned parents, we had him tested and found out he had a very high I.Q. School officials facetiously said he belonged in the eleventh grade. The social problems inherent in such a solution were obvious, so we kept him home and hired a private tutor.

With two parents in show biz, it was natural that Butch would get involved. He started while we lived in Los Angeles. Ben Hunter, one of my friends, was a KTTV show host who produced several shows for Metromedia. He was going to produce a news show for children, using kids, and wanted Butch as one of the anchors. Butch was prepared to do it. At the age of seven he was reading a teleprompter and cold copy, that is, looking down at papers and up at the camera without losing his place. That is even difficult for many adults. But the 1971 Castaic earthquake (6.6) hit, and we decided to leave the area.

By the time he was nine, we were living at Dunlap and he was ready for the Fresno market. Al Radka, an old-time Fresno personality, had run the United Cerebral Palsy telethon in Fresno for years. Butch went on Radka's show for three of those years. Al became a good friend of ours.

From there, Butch went to radio. Von Johnson, now with Disney Cable in Burbank, California, was then at Channel 30 and was also working for KVPR, the local public radio station. He gave twelve-year-old Butch the task of getting interviews for the station. In the next year and a half Butch "was thrust," as he says, "into a career, not a training stage." He got interviews, all right, exclusive reports that the networks didn't get. These, in turn, got him admitted to places where most twelve- and thirteen-year-olds couldn't dream of entering. I think there were two underlying reasons for his success. He was good at interviews and he was an excellent flim-flam man. He could talk people into giving him entry into all kinds of places. And he'd just say "hello" to an interviewee, it seemed, and the person would start in on a life story.

Butch's stories and his contacts brought him lots of media attention. By the time he was sixteen he had been written about in *US* magazine, the Sacramento *Record-Union* and the Fresno *Bee*, and had been reported on by CBS News and United Press International.

Butch wasn't aware that his successes were sparking professional jealousy among some of the adults. They complained to the station manager, who went to Butch and hinted that he might be out.

Undaunted, Butch asked, "What if I can get an interview with Kirk Douglas?"

"If you can get the interview," the manager said with skepticism, "you can stay on the show."

The next day Butch handed in the interview.

After that came interviews with Jack Lemmon, Mike Douglas, the NASA astronauts (minus Neil Armstrong and Buzz Aldrin), and Kirk Douglas' sons.

During the 1978 Christmas season, Butch was able to get recorded Christmas messages from such notables as Pope John Paul II; President Carter; Linda Steinberg of the United Nations; President Carter's assistant press secretary Jim Purks; Fresno's Democratic Congressman Tony Coelho; actor and comedian George Gobel; TV game show host Peter Marshall; mimic Frank Gorshin; and Bob Barker, host of *The Price Is Right* and *Truth or Consequences*.

Linda Steinberg appointed Butch the youth representative of UNICEF. He did a lot of promotional work for that organization, for which he received a certificate from the UN. He got more celebrity interviews: singers Ray Charles, Ray Stevens, and B.J. Thomas.

I don't think it went to Butch's head. He developed a tough

hide from seeing Hollywood agents and producers get into fist fights, then go out together for a friendly drink. He learned from our lives and experiences that there could be a love-hate relationship with agents and producers.

Butch knew terms like "close-up" and "wide shot" because of us. I got him a segment with Al Radka at KFSN when he was fourteen. There he did five minutes of news items called "Butch's Corner," a series of generic news and star interviews. Radka's show was *Saturday Children's Showcase* on which grammar school students sang or danced. This was entertaining to the children and parents, but it was boring to everyone else. The FCC required an hour of free children's programming each week and this rule had to be strictly adhered to. Walt Liss, the station manager, became tired of the show. He offered me an opportunity to produce a new children's show with Bob Versace, the production manager, and Robbie Robinson, the studio director. It was a different type of children's show, one with segments that included Butch's news, the zoo, exercises, cooking, the county library, and science experiments. For humor, we would use clips of Lee Azhderian (a Dunlap neighbor) spinning yarns about the mountains.

Polly helped me by contributing from her wealth of ideas. The new program was called *Valley Main Street* and was set in a town where Al Radka was the mayor, and Butch was his enterprising journalist-nephew. They went on location to interesting nearby places. It was a shoestring operation that we all really believed in, so we worked extra hours without pay. Butch would run it.

Our pilot was the test and featured the Circus Vargas. Butch's interview with the lion tamer proved to be super and everyone was delighted.

There was another show at the time, *360*, a half-hour news magazine that preceeded *60 Minutes* and therefore had built-in ratings. The *360* show had four field producers, two full-time photographers and a bountiful budget. They had no problem getting their material ready from week to week. We, on the other hand, had a small budget, a skeleton crew, had to rent a cameraman, and were six weeks ahead on locations.

We made twenty-six weeks of shows and then re-ran those to make twenty-six more. Everyone who worked on our show was proud of it.

Someone complained to Liss that Butch was benefitting from nepotism. Liss had no choice but to let Butch go. However, Butch had received eighteen months of opportunity and experience and had used the time well.

Butch's interviews led to an interest in government, which enabled him to obtain fantastic contacts. He became a good friend of our local congressmen, Democrat Tony Coelho and Republican Chip Pashayan; Democratic National Committee Chairman Robert Strauss; Jimmy Carter's assistant press secretary, Jim Purks; Carter's son, Chip; and Ronald Reagan's press secretary, James Brady.

Butch was seventeen years old when Reagan and Brady were shot. Butch was scheduling an interview with Reagan through Brady for that very morning. After the initial hubbub passed and it was apparent the President would survive, Butch got in touch with Elizabeth Dole to offer his assistance. He gave an autographed picture of me with my tough kid expression to Nancy Reagan to give to the President as soon as he was out of intensive care. Later, when he was recovering at Santa Barbara, President Reagan wrote to thank us personally for the laughter the picture elicited.

After *Valley Main Street*, Butch got an assignment from the Fresno Unified School District to create thirteen segments interviewing prominent visitors to Fresno. The program was called *School Reel*. Among those he reached were Dennis Morgan, Ken Curtis (Festus of *Gunsmoke*), Richard Keel, John Houseman, and the Lennon Sisters.

Then Butch embarked on a new project, the movie *Clingan's Junction*. It was about a town in Virginia where residents chose to live in the past, in 1863, pre-Civil War, in the hopes that they would realize their past mistakes and that the Civil War would not be repeated. What a production! He formed a company, Bond Productions, and brought in photographer Bob Tyrcha, actors and actresses, and 120 extras (many of whom were locals). They used the Pioneer Village in Selma, a nearby community. They had a cherry picker, which served as a boom for the camera, and the crew made and rented costumes. The amount of free help couldn't possibly be calculated. The movie was shot in fourteen days over a period from 1982 to 1984. Many newspapers covered the project, and movie reviewers declared that *Clingan's Junction* had meaning, depth, and impact. It was shown at a sneak preview at Warnor's theatre in Fresno.

So why haven't you seen it?

On St. Patrick's Day, 1985, a propane tank exploded at our Dunlap ranch. The house and the tape master were destroyed, as were many mementos and records of our lives. Worse, Polly's mother and sister were burned terribly and were in critical condition for quite some time. Thank God, they recovered. Their recovery was aided in great part by the wonderful staff of the Valley Medical Center's burn unit in Fresno.

That disaster prompted our move to Fresno and, later in 1987, to rural Madera County, north of Fresno. There I indulged in my love for the soil, planted my own corn and salad vegetables, and raised hens for eggs.

As for Butch, he's doing just fine. He has his own corporation, Biograph Pictures.

I retired in 1991, though I didn't have to. Channel 30 was good to me, helping my retirement portfolio grow through a profit-sharing plan and by investing additional amounts in securities. So, why did I retire? Simple. I wanted to go fishing.

Memory Lane

There have been fan clubs since the early days of filmdom. Individual actors or actresses, producers or directors, movies or series have inspired the viewing public to organize in order to keep the object of their devotion figuratively alive and well. One such worthy group is the Sons of the Desert.

The Sons of the Desert was organized in 1964 by Stan Laurel and his biographer, John McCabe, to preserve the memory of Laurel and Hardy. The first meetings were held in New York City's Lambs Club in mid-1965, shortly after Laurel died. By mid-1992 there were more than 150 "tents," or chapters, worldwide.

The Sons have amply fulfilled their original intent, collecting every scrap of material relating to "the boys" and by maintaining meticulous records in Universal City, near Los

Angeles. If you have a question about the comedy team, Sons of the Desert has the answer.

They're not only record-keepers, they help those in need as well. Anyone who was in a Laurel and Hardy movie and who has fallen on hard times need only contact the Sons, and help is on its way. It's a great organization and one that can move mountains, because it represents a genre of entertainment that will live forever. Does that sound like a bold statement? I could tone it down somewhat by saying that it will live as long as there's a kid left in any of us.

Some great movers and shakers belong to the Sons of the Desert. The Way Out West Tent, formed in 1967 by ex-detective Bill Patterson, includes Lori Jones, long-time secretary; Bob Satterfield, the former Grand Sheik; and Lois and Tony Hawes, daughter and son-in-law of Stan Laurel. These are just a few of the names that come to mind.

Shortly before her death, Darla Hood approached the Sons and suggested that the other Roach comedy team, the *Gang*, be added to their honored legends. They liked the idea. Laurel and Hardy remain foremost in the Sons' devotion, but the *Gang* is there too, receiving the same caring for their welfare and verification as that given to "the boys."

Darla died before the 1980 reunion which brought all of us old *Gang*-sters together again. Bob Satterfield called to invite me to the reunion. Dwelling on the past never was my cup of tea, but he persisted. Polly and I agreed to go. Butch was in the middle of his *Valley Main Street* show, so we went on the premise that he would conduct interviews with the *Gang* attendees and air the clips on his program. His audience would enjoy it. So away we went.

Reunions create unanticipated bonds between people. On our arrival at the Hilton Hotel in Los Angeles Bob Satterfield told me, "I want you to meet someone who's an old friend of yours."

It was Spanky, and it was a most emotional moment. Spanky and I had never been close in the old days, but our meeting brought us together warmly after forty years. We hugged and cried like brothers. I think the closeness arose from reminiscing together. Now, as adults, we sat and recalled the old days — who did what and to whom.

Spanky had a lovely family — wife, son, and daughter. He had been hurt when Hollywood ignored him after he left the *Gang*. Over the years he played a few minor roles, but he did not continue with a movie career. He headed home to Texas where he found his career as sales manager for Kitchen Aid in Fort Worth. There he retired. His most recent role was as an 1890s Texas governor in *The Aurora Encounter* (1987), the story of a little spaceman's visit to a small town.

Spanky had mellowed. Still as opinionated and demonstrative as ever, he nevertheless had become much warmer. We got together every two years after that reunion. And then, on July 1, 1993, he suffered a cardiac arrest. As soon as I heard the news I telephoned his wife Doris. She told me he had passed away peacefully.

Another fellow I hadn't seen in years was Buckwheat. He enjoyed seeing himself on the screen and loved the reunions. His eyes filled with tears as he confessed to our Butch, Jr., who was interviewing him, "I haven't had so much fun in years, with us all back together."

About six months later I received a call at about 11 p.m. from John Wallace, who was still KFSN's news anchor.

"I have something to tell you," he opened. "Remember that interview your son did with Buckwheat?"

"Yes?" I instinctively knew what was coming.

"Well, I hate to tell you this, but he passed away. I need some footage. Can I use a clip from your *Main Street* show? It's the last known interview he gave."

"Of course," I assured him. I was quite broken up. Buckwheat was such a nice, sweet human being.

One of the other African-American child actors couldn't make it to the reunion. Allen "Farina" Hoskins had cancer and died the next year. Buckwheat, Farina, and Stymie had all died within a year of each other.

On a happier note, after I met Spanky at the reunion, Bob Satterfield asked if I remembered Dorothy DeBorba who played Echo.

"Of course!"

"You're going to meet her next."

She was staying in the room across from ours. Bob and I knocked on her door. A mature woman with sparkling eyes and cane in hand, answered our knock and it was tears all over again. Dorothy also loved reunions. As she told Butch, "They're wonderful — Christmas, Easter, and birthdays all rolled into one!" She hasn't missed any of them. Dorothy lives in Livermore, California, near Oakland. She retains her sharp wit, a wonderful sense of humor, and has a great outlook on life.

Another old friend I saw at the '80 reunion was Sid Kibrick, "the Woim." He'd changed from a freckle-faced kid into a tall, handsome man. Polly couldn't get over how great he looked. He had continued to act for a few years after the *Gang* days. Then he joined his brother, Leonard, and has been successful in the real estate business.

In 1986 he called to invite us to visit Palm Springs.

"I have a *Little Rascals* clubhouse that I've built at my RV center, with lots of old pictures and artifacts. I want all the main *Gang* members to put their handprints and footprints in concrete to last forever."

It sounded good, so we went down and had a marvelous time. My red-haired, freckle-faced sidekick had done very well for himself. Another great guy.

Some years before, while I was still at KTTV, I got a call from Jackie Taylor, who had played with me in the *Gang's Hi'-Neighbor!*

"I hope you remember me, Tommy. I played in *Our Gang* with you. My husband and I are ministers in the Unity Church in San Diego."

Of course I remembered her. She had been with the *Little Rascals* for the 1934 season. She was interested in reviving public interest in the *Gang* and wanted to know if I could help in some way. I was agreeable.

After a period of time, she came and interviewed me, and used clips of the interview on her show. She co-hosted the show with Stymie and Johnny Downs, a *Gang* member from the early days. Downs, now retired, had his own kiddie show in San Diego.

Again I heard nothing more from her for years. Her next call was an invitation to participate in a new series she was putting together for a Reno station. It would consist of nineteen shows. A very talented woman, she had written a book called *Jackie Remembers Our Gang*. She did a great deal of research on the *Gang* members (I would tend to believe her in any dispute about their fates). The show would promote the book and other things kids might like, with interviews, film clips, and a lot of talk about the *Gang*. It sounded good.

"We could do the outside stuff at your ranch and then we'll go to Reno and tape the studio stuff there," she said. "It'll air in Reno."

That sounded okay to me. They came down, we taped all the exteriors, and three weeks later she asked me to bring my family to Reno. Polly, Butch, and I went, and over a week's time I helped her with ten shows in a recreated Clubhouse.

179

One who wasn't at the 1980 reunion was Porky. But if he had been, Bob Satterfield would have had to introduce us. If the Woim had changed, you had to have seen Porky. Today, Gordon Lee is six feet two inches, bearded, and nothing like the little moon-faced kid I remembered. Whenever he joined us for subsequent reunions or interviews, people just didn't believe he was Porky. While Spanky and I were recognizable, he'd have to swear up and down that Gordon and Porky were one and the same.

Others who have shown up at reunions include Waldo, Mickey, and Junior. That's the beauty of Sons of the Desert — they've brought into the light what was in the darkness.

Waldo (Darwood K. Smith) is a Seventh-Day Adventist minister in the Midwest, a fine gentleman. He was awed when called by the Sons. Mickey is now the actor Robert Blake. He played in a number of movies and starred in the TV series *Barretta*. Junior (Mel Jasgar) is a very good friend who's grown from the dead-pan little boy into the owner of a sauna manufacturing plant in Los Angeles. He really enjoyed himself at the 1986 Palm Springs, California, reunion.

Gang members are not the only ones who attend these reunions. At one reunion in Los Angeles, Polly and I were at the dinner table when I looked up and saw Eileen Barton, known in earlier times as Jolly Gillette. She had been Milton Berle's teenage girl protégé, with a terrific voice like Judy Garland's or Eydie Gorme's. Jolly sang in intervals between Berle's various comedy schticks in his radio show, *Gillette Community Sings*, and the audience sang along with her.

I'd like to tell you about two 1986 reunions: the one in Palm Springs and the other in San Antonio.

We met at Palm Springs in February. Two Leonards were there: Kibrick and Maltin (the writer). Maltin reunited a number of us, including Dorothy DeBorba, Porky, Spanky, Sunshine Sammy, Junior, and the Smith Brothers. We all put our hands in concrete at Sid's Clubhouse.

The Smith Brothers? The bearded men on the cough drop box? No. They were Richard and Robert, twins who started with the *Gang* in 1927 and eventually went on to W.C. Fields and Will Rogers comedies. They retired as sheriff's deputies for Fresno County.

Heidi Mitchell, working for Channel 6, Palm Springs, interviewed us old-timers who were planning at least one more reunion before heading for the big clubhouse in the sky. It was an international gathering and a gathering of old memories.

Robert Blake recalled how child actors had fallen into hay balers and off fire engines, and would protect one another to prevent competitor actors from moving in and taking over.

Also in attendance were the Woim, Pineapple Jackson, Jackie Taylor, and Marvin Hatley, who wrote many Roach theme songs, though not the *Gang*'s "Good Old Days." Our theme song had been written by LeRoy Shield, who in 1930 and 1931 wrote a number of the catchy background themes used in the Roach shorts. Hatley wrote the famous Laurel and Hardy theme song, which he called "Coo-Coo." The Roach studio retitled it "Ku Ku" and re-copyrighted it in an attempt to cheat Marvin out of royalties! Thankfully, he was able to regain ownership of the tune in the mid-1950s.

What did the ever-talkative Spanky have to say? Only that no single individual other than Roach was responsible for the show's success.

Dennis Du Priest, a San Antonio teacher and a big fan of the *Rascals*, arranged the reunion in San Antonio. He organized a personal appearance for Spanky, Porky, and me. Again, the climax was hands in concrete, this time at the Westlake Theater in San Antonio. There was a good deal of TV coverage. To the media folks Geri Jarvis and Richard Noriega of

KSAT and Gary DeLaune, "the innocence of youth transcends time."

Porky, then a teacher in Boulder, Colorado, was probably the center of attention at that reunion, for he was busily engaged in getting legislative protection for older stars to prevent their exploitation. California's "Celebrity Rights Act," part of civil codes 990 and 3344, is an example of such legislation.

Clowns, midgets, and dwarf actors felt a curious kinship with those of us who were child actors. Many of the Munchkin midgets in *Oz* went on to clowning in circuses or in the movies.

In 1986 I was at the circus with co-workers from Channel 30 when a group of little people grabbed me and took me backstage.

"What's going on?" I demanded.

"Butch," their leader, Kevin Thompson, answered, "you're one of our idols. We have a *Little Rascals* fan club. Would you talk to us about your days with the *Rascals*?"

I've never had a kinder, nicer, more fun-loving audience. They related to the *Little Rascals* because they were little and they still saw us as little.

Even today's kids don't want to accept the fact that any of the kids in the *Gang* are old or dead. Today's children, as well as those of yesterday and the day before, see us/them as children, alive and kicking.

When Roach discontinued production of the *Our Gang* series in 1938, he sold the title to MGM. What followed was a mass of legal confusion, as Roach re-acquired and re-assigned, and other companies sprang up and collapsed. The series was, in the words of Maltin and Bann in their book *Our Gang*, "kicked around through more irresponsible hands than a park grounds football." King World Productions began distributing the series to TV in 1955.

Maybe nostalgia might stir a ripple of enthusiasm for the fourth *Gang* (post-me) group and their films, for nothing else will, due in part to the local independent television stations that air the films today. Let's face it, air time is expensive, and the stations are interested in selling time. If they could get away with ninety-nine percent commercials and one percent other uses, they would do it. But they can't. So they run old films, syndicated programs — whatever — and they butcher them. They chop them unmercifully to permit the maximum number of commercials. Artistic editing goes out the window, and the story is distorted.

From the time I started with the *Gang*, funny things have been a part of my life. I've been told I've retained the sense of humor that got me through the *Gang* days. There's some kid in all of us.

Part of my philosophy of life is that if you can't get a laugh out of it, what good is it? If you go through life without a sense of humor or without appreciating others who have a sense of humor, life can be very drab. Life is enriched by laughter.

One problem that happens with some actors and actresses is the imposter. The imposter problem took up much of the five years Maltin and Bann needed to get their book about the *Gang* completed.

Richard Lamparsky wrote *Where Are They Now?* In that book someone other than Gordon Lee claimed to be Porky. The imposter presented himself with confidence and even provided a picture. Lamparsky didn't check him out thoroughly the first time. Gordon, the real Porky, was livid. He showed Lamparsky the proof that he was, indeed, Porky, and in the following edition the error was corrected. Still, the imposter denied any wrongdoing.

Lamparsky really can't be blamed. Who would have guessed that anyone would claim to be Porky? Or Spanky? Or me, Butch?

Spanky had some real problems with imposters. Once a man used his name, filled out a tax return under his name, and then did not pay his taxes. Spanky got a call from the IRS and was told that he was in arrears on taxes, and that he had taken other people's money for a tax shelter and used it illegally. The burden of proof was on Spanky. It was a very bad experience, but Spanky finally cleared up the confusion.

When I was at KTTV I got a call from a high school friend I hadn't seen in years. He worked with the bunko squad. When he arrived at the studio we chatted for a while and then he got to the point.

"Do you remember Spanky?"

"Yeah." Rule number one is "Don't commit yourself."

"Is Spanky living in Hawaii?"

"I haven't seen him in years. I think he's living in Texas."

"Well," he held up a picture, "does this look like him?"

The photograph showed a man with an uncanny resemblance to Spanky. I jumped to the clinching evidence. "How tall is this guy?"

"He's six feet two inches," came the reply.

"That's not Spanky."

Apparently, a heavy-set man who bore a resemblance to Spanky was operating a Hawaiian porno ring and my old friend, the agent, needed to confirm or reject the identification. He thanked me and left.

I didn't have any problems until I moved to Fresno County, and then I had two beauties.

One day at KFSN an interesting item came over the AP wire and one of the producers called me over.

"Look at this, Tom. It just came over the wire: Gabby Hayes' son was interviewed in Colorado last week. He was the original Butch in the *The Our Gang Comedies*. His name at that time was Tommy Bond. Blah-blah-blah."

Gloria Moraga, a feisty newswoman who liked me, was our weekend anchor and wanted to set things straight. She called the TV station in Denver and asked about the man who claimed to be both Gabby Hayes' son and me. They gave her his phone number. She called him.

"Hello. Is this Tommy Bond? You're Gabby Hayes' son? Your name is really Tommy Bond and you were Butch in the *Little Rascals*?"

He answered "yes" to all her questions. Then she let the other shoe drop.

"That's funny. I have the real Tommy Bond standing next to me, and he'd like to have a few words with you."

The poor fool started babbling and mumbling, and she followed up with a right cross.

"If we ever, ever hear of any more impersonation, you will be prosecuted." She wasn't finished. "Now, when I get through talking to you, I'm going to call the Denver press and TV and set them straight."

She did just that and we never heard another word about

it. Obviously, he never dreamed he'd be caught.

About six months later I was in the station coffee shop when the phone rang and Eva, our receptionist, told me, "Tom, you have a long-distance call."

Over the phone came the voice of a Southern woman.

"I want to know," she began, "if I'm talking to the Tommy Bond who played Butch in *The Little Rascals*."

"Yes. How did you find me?"

She had tracked me down through multiple phone calls. She poured out what has unfortunately become a not uncommon story. It seemed that her wealthy father was senile. He always loved *The Our Gang Comedies*. An evangelist got to him and won his trust by telling him that he, the evangelist, was Butch. He persuaded her father to invest in one of his schemes. She tried to tell her father that the man was an imposter, but he wouldn't believe her. She needed proof and contacting me seemed to satisfy her.

There were other claims, more or less harmless, though annoying.

At a reunion in San Jose, California, I was fielding a question-and-answer session when one fellow asked about "the second Alfalfa." I dropped my upper plate. "Wait a minute. There was no second Alfalfa. There was only one Alfalfa. Where did you get that idea?"

He told me that he'd heard of a man who claimed to be the second Alfalfa.

"Let's get one thing straight," I began. "There was only one Alfalfa, one Spanky, one Porky, one Darla, and one Butch. If you have any doubts about who is who, you can always contact the Sons of the Desert."

In 1990, ten years after Buckwheat died, a grocery bagger in Tucson, Arizona, passed himself off to the TV investigative program *20/20* as Buckwheat. Immediately *20/20* was set straight, but why hadn't one of the program's fact checkers done some quick homework? The producer of the segment resigned.

I don't think characters like Darla Hood, Joe Cobb, or Jackie Cooper were impersonated. If they were, it didn't materialize into anything significant. For example, a man claimed to be the character "Stinky." There never was a Stinky. It was a relatively harmless claim because no one's identity was robbed, and it was only half a claim to fame. But it was pathetic, wasn't it?

Fame carries with it a certain security, but it can also be a liability. The bright side of all this is that probably you'll only be impersonated if you are famous. If fame is what you want, consider this: It is transitory? I could have gone through life happily without it. What makes me happy? Enjoying life, having a loving family, and making good friends.

Something I've learned over the years — put life in God's care. When I made the move from KTTV to Dunlap and Fresno, there were ups and downs. But the good Lord guided us the right way. I think He has opened doors for me and said, "Get your foot in it. This is the way to go." If you're smart, you follow that lead. If there's a closed door, try another one — because He doesn't want you to enter that first one. It's the open door that presents you with the opportunity. If it's closed, it's closed; you have to accept that. There's a reason for everything. You may not see the positive aspects of an experience while it is happening, but eventually you will. Realize this and you'll be happier.

The *Gang* reunions are still a lot of fun, but there are fewer of us each time.

On the morning of November 2, 1992, I received a phone

call from Dan Taylor, a friend at Channel 30.

"Tom," he started, "I hate to tell you this, but Hal Roach died this morning."

Hal was one hundred, and so it was expected, though you're never ready for that kind of news. He was the last of the movie moguls. When Mr. Roach died, I realized that the Golden Years of Hollywood were truly over. The years I grew up in . . . the great movie moguls . . . Mervyn LeRoy, Frank Capra, L.B. Mayer, Sam Goldwyn, the Warners . . . all the producers I knew and knew of . . . all gone now.

Mr. Roach is gone, too, along with our childhood and youth. But our history and those wonderful memories can never be taken from us. They will always live in the memories of the young at heart.

Filmography*

1932
Spanky (Roach) — The Our Gang Comedies

1933
Forgotten Babies (Roach) - The Our Gang Comedies
The Kid From Borneo (Roach) - The Our Gang Comedies
Mush and Milk (Roach) - The Our Gang Comedies
Bedtime Worries (Roach) - The Our Gang Comedies
Wild Poses (Roach) - The Our Gang Comedies
Hi'-Neighbor! (Roach) - The Our Gang Comedies
I'll Take Vanilla (Roach) - Charlie Chase
For Pete's Sake (Roach) - The Our Gang Comedies
The First Round-Up (Roach) - The Our Gang Comedies
Honky Donkey (Roach) - The Our Gang Comedies
Mike Fright (Roach) - The Our Gang Comedies
Washee Ironee (Roach) - The Our Gang Comedies

1934
Kid Millions (Goldwyn) - Feature

1935
Alimony Aches (Columbia) - Andy Clyde Comedies

1936
Hideaway (RKO) - Feature
Next Time We Love (Universal) - Feature
Monty Collins—Tom Kennedy Comedies (Columbia)
Glove Taps (Roach) - Our Gang Comedies

*Dates reflect when the movies were produced.

1937

Knee Action (Columbia) - Andy Clyde Comedies
Rosalie (MGM) - Feature
Rushin' Ballet (Roach) - The Our Gang Comedies
Fishy Tales (Roach) - The Our Gang Comedies
Framing Youth (Roach) - The Our Gang Comedies
Came the Brawn (Roach) - The Our Gang Comedies

1938

City Streets (Columbia) - Feature
Blockheads (Roach) - with Laurel & Hardy
The Little Ranger (MGM) - Our Gang
Party Fever (MGM) - Our Gang
Football Romeo (MGM) - Our Gang
Practical Jokers (MGM) - Our Gang

1935-1938

Don't Look Now (Warner) - Cartoon voice
Mr. & Mrs. Is the Name (Warner) - Cartoon voice
My Green Fedora (Warner) - Cartoon voice
I'd Love to Take Orders From You (Warner) - Cartoon voice
I Love to Sing (Warner) - Cartoon voice
I Wanna Be a Sailor (Warner) - Cartoon voice
The Major Lied 'Til Dawn (Warner) - Cartoon voice

1939

Duel Personalities (MGM) - Our Gang
Cousin Wilbur (MGM) - Our Gang
Dog Daze (MGM) - Our Gang
Let's Talk Turkey (MGM) - Pete Smith short
Auto Antics (MGM) - Our Gang

Captain Spanky's Showboat (MGM) - Our Gang
Now It Can Be Sold (Columbia) - Andy Clyde Comedies
Five Little Peppers (Columbia) - Feature

1940
Bubbling Troubles (MGM) - Our Gang
Five Little Peppers at Home (Columbia) - Feature
Out West With the Peppers (Columbia) - Feature
Five Little Peppers in Trouble (Columbia) - Feature
A Little Bit of Heaven (Universal) - Feature

1941
Adventures in Washington (Columbia) - Feature

1943
This Land is Mine (RKO) - Feature
Man From Frisco (Republic) - Feature

1944
Twice Blessed (MGM) - Feature

1946
Superman vs the Spider Lady (Columbia) -Serial

1947
Big Town Scandal (Pine-Thomas) - Feature
Gas House Kids Go West (PRC) - Feature
Gas House Kids in Hollywood (PRC) - Feature

1948
Atom Man vs. Superman (Columbia) - Serial

1949

Any Number Can Play (MGM) - Feature

Battleground (MGM) - Feature

Tokyo Joe (Columbia) - Feature

1950

Hot Rod (PRC) - Feature

1951

Call Me Mister (20th Century) - Feature